ON
THIS
PATCH
OF
GRASS

ON THIS PATCH OF GRASS

City Parks on Occupied Land

Daisy Couture, Sadie Couture, Selena Couture and Matt Hern

With Denise Ferreira da Silva, Glen Coulthard, Erick Villagomez

Fernwood Publishing
Halifax & Winnipeg

Editing: Fazeela Jiwa and Brenda Conroy
Text design: Brenda Conroy
Cover images: Hal Ozart and Zac Sturgeon
Cover design: Tania Craan
Printed and bound in Canada

Published by Fernwood Publishing
32 Oceanvista Lane, Black Point, Nova Scotia, B0J 1B0
and 748 Broadway Avenue, Winnipeg, Manitoba, R3G 0X3
www.fernwoodpublishing.ca

Fernwood Publishing Company Limited gratefully acknowledges the financial support of the Government of Canada, the Manitoba Department of Culture, Heritage and Tourism under the Manitoba Publishers Marketing Assistance Program and the Province of Manitoba, through the Book Publishing Tax Credit, for our publishing program. We are pleased to work in partnership with the Province of Nova Scotia to develop and promote our creative industries for the benefit of all Nova Scotians. We acknowledge the support of the Canada Council for the Arts, which last year invested $153 million to bring the arts to Canadians throughout the country.

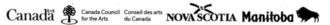

Library and Archives Canada Cataloguing in Publication

On this patch of grass: city parks on occupied land / Daisy
Couture, Sadie Couture, Selena Couture and Matt Hern with Denise
Ferreira da Silva, Glen Coulthard, Erick Villagomez

Includes bibliographical references.
Issued in print and electronic formats.
ISBN 978-1-77363-070-0 (softcover).—ISBN 978-1-77363-071-7 (EPUB).—
ISBN 978-1-77363-072-4 (Kindle)

1. Urban parks—Political aspects—British Columbia—Vancouver.
2. Urban parks—Social aspects—British Columbia—Vancouver.
I. Hern, Matt, 1968-. Building better landscapes

FC3847.65.O5 2018   363.6'80971133   C2018-903708-3
C2018-904498-5

CONTENTS

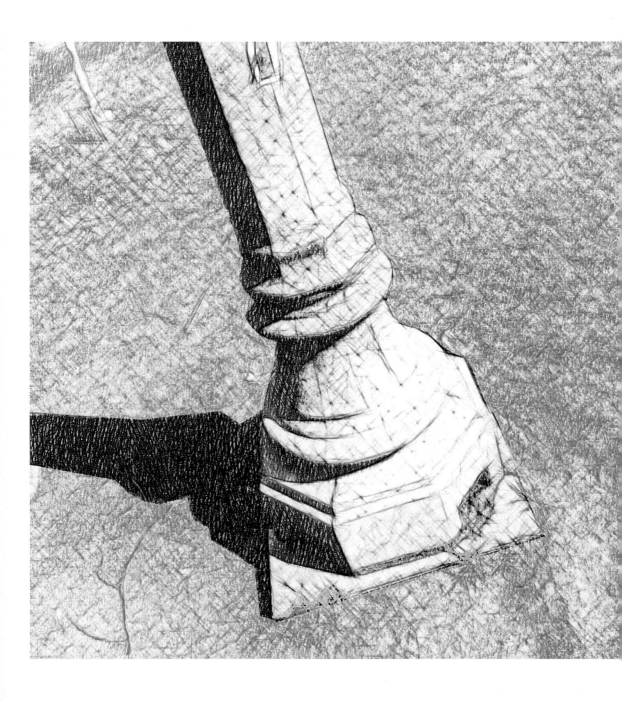

ACKNOWLEDGEMENTS

In some ways, this whole book is an expression of gratitude and love for where we live and the people and the other-than-humans we live amongst. We do want to note though some of the people who specifically helped us in the creation of this book.

First, thanks as always, to our immediate neighbours and the many, many others who have lived here, beside and with us, over the all these years. Our love goes to the wider group of dear friends who make living in this city worth it. You know who you are, and with luck you will hear some of your voices in here.

Second, our gratitude is owed to Glen Coulthard, Denise Ferreira da Silva, Erick Villagomez and everyone who was interviewed for this book. Without all your voices, this book would be impossible.

Third, our thanks go to Fernwood Publishing for their generous support of this complicated hybrid work; especially to Candida Hadley for her kind attentiveness, patience and incisive thinking, and to Beverley Rach, Fazeela Jiwa and Brenda Conroy for their forbearance as we assembled all the pieces.

And finally, much love to our families, extended and otherwise — on Vancouver Island, Ontario, and scattered widely — for their continuing care and love and cynicism.

Foreword

THE COLONIAL RESIDENT QUESTION

Having lived in this particular corner of the Pacific Northwest, on the Musqueam First Nation Reserve, for three years, recently I found myself walking along the trails in Pacific Spirit Park with a feeling — yes, I do mean feeling — that there is something I will never grasp. Though I do not recall precisely how it was when I did not have this feeling, I do know that it was not there at first. It came later, slowly, and became more intense the more I became used to the beauty of the forest, the gentle but indelible summer light seeping through the trees, the rugged grounds with fallen leaves, the muddy paths, filled with puddles, in the winter, the first touches of colour that announce spring. Every time I walk on these ancestral Musqueam grounds, this stretch of temperate rain forest greets me as a recently arrived colonial resident (a settler) who was born and raised in a city also built on colonized lands. It gifts me with a different kind of appreciation for the question that, to me, permeates this family's love letter to this city and its ancestral custodians and colonial residents (settlers). I call it the colonial resident question.

The colonial resident question was — and still is — postponed. When it does surface, it comes to thought later: after the questioning of capital, after racial redress, after ... but it rarely does. For the classic historical materialists, the colonial question is not even about to become relevant — not even after something was accomplished or a phase was completed. Nor had it a place in the political imaginary that animated the several lines of critical political discourse of the local and national struggles — communist, socialist, anti-racist, feminist, pro-LGBTI — that is, the whole gamut of political movements that consolidated in the 1980s. These movements for social justice addressed the state under the assumption that it had the right to exist, that all that was needed was that the state included the rest of us, namely, the poor, Black, female, gay folks.

It is not that means of colonialization (conquest and slavery) have not been part of that political vocabulary. They have been. What is lacking is a formulation of the colonial resident question precisely because it immediately and instantaneously challenges that which these political movements want to accomplish by being heard by the state.

Now it is not a matter of finding a "proper" formulation of the question and all will be well, and the left/radical/critical/progressive political discourse will be finally complete. This is not a matter of time. Nor is it a matter of inclusion. The colonial resident question extends beyond the conceptual and existential elements comprehended by the modern political text.

What then? Reading *On this Patch of Grass*, I found myself, in several moments, thinking about whether or not it makes sense to try and articulate, as a question, the complications, contradictions and complexities of a political existence of the kind experienced by the colonial resident. Perhaps what we need is not so much another version of the political discourse but a different kind of composition — a fragmentary and yet directed and intended one, which like Daisy, Sadie, Selena and Matt's book, presents the colonial resident question with all its difficulties and without apology.

It may not meet the criteria of the political discourse; actually, it may fail it all together. Ethically and aesthetically, however, such composition might just get us a bit closer to the goal. For only such a composition — as a kind of text that articulates but does not resolve everything back in to a political position — might accommodate the ethical mandate to call into question our own existence, the one this book exposes so well. For there is a double demand to colonial residents, to all of us settlers who are defined by the feeling of never grasping the land: do not reproduce the violence and violations that render our living in occupied lands possible *and* that we support and, if invited, join in the struggle for returning the lands (and all the wealth expropriated from them since conquest) to their ancestral guardians, the Squamish, Tsleil-Waututh and Musqueam First Nations, the ones who feel this land in all its fullness because they are one with it.

— *Denise Ferreira da Silva, professor and director of the*
Institute for Gender, Race, Sexuality and Social Justice,
University of British Columbia

1

CITY PARKS ON
OCCUPIED LAND

Is there *no* burden for the "descendant of colonial peoples"? Are there no burdens associated ... being descended from those who have committed crimes against humanity, or living off the avails of these crimes? To deny this burden is to withhold a crucial truth; to refuse to shoulder and show this burden is to remain a bystander. (Carter 2015: 423–24)

Victoria Park, day 1. Photo by Daisy Couture

This is a book about parks and how parks act on stolen land. It is a book about occupation, which we mean in both senses: first, the occupation of Indigenous land by settlers, and second, how parks are occupied by pluralities of users. Our submission here is that thinking closely about the latter can shed some light on the former; that is, looking carefully at what parks do — how they behave and how they are deployed in cities — offers unique opportunities to catch a glimpse of a decolonial horizon.

Parks are particularly fertile places to talk about land. Whether referring to national parks, provincial campgrounds, isolated conservation areas, destination parks or humble urban patches of grass, people tend to speak of parks as unqualified good things — maybe the best possible use of land. It is easy to think of parks as land that makes all of us better.

But no park is innocent. Parks are lionized as "natural" oases, and urban parks are often spoken of as "nature" in the midst of the city — but that's absurd. Parks, urban or not, are exactly as "natural" as the roads or buildings around them, and they are just as political. Every park in North America is performing modernity and settler colonialism on an everyday basis. Parks occupy all kinds of middle grounds: they are not private property, they are called "public" places, and they are highly regulated. People like to think of parks as part of the "commons," but they normatively demand and closely control behaviours.

Cities are defined by land management policies; they discipline movement and demarcate who can occupy which space, why, where, how and when. Parks are a certain kind of property — usually owned by a level of the state and thus creations of law — but they are also subject to all kinds of cultural presumptions about what they are for and what kinds of people should be doing what kinds of things in them. Parks as they are currently constituted are always colonial enterprises.

As four white settlers living on səlil̓wətaʔɬ (Tsleil-Waututh), Sḵwx̱wú7mesh (Squamish) and xʷməθkʷəy̓əm (Musqueam) territory, we are interested in our relationships with this land and how to we might challenge and change our modes of living as colonial visitors. We encounter parks in everyday and bodily senses, and most particularly, we encounter one small park beside our house every day: Victoria Park, known mostly as Bocce Ball Park. This book is one small attempt to confront our colonial attitudes toward land and to remake our relationships with parks, especially Victoria Park. There are four threads entwined in this project:

1. The first thread considers the uses and histories of parks (and specifically Bocce Ball Park) to understand and complicate how they have been, and are, deployed. We want to throw the occupation of parks into doubt.
2. The second piece notes the complicity of parks in creating and regulating narratives of control and domination that are bound up with race, class and gender. Parks, including Bocce Ball Park, are inflected heavily by performances of whiteness, and we want to continually poke at that.
3. At the same time, parks are key instruments of settler colonialism. Parks make arguments about the occupation of land and, as such, are colonial exercises. We ask how parks — and Bocce Ball Park in particular — actively construct colonial relations.
4. Finally, we are curious about how parks, and Bocce Ball Park especially, can be remade. Much is laudable about parks, and we are especially interested in how the overlapping and shared uses, the malleable sovereignties and the fluidity of parks might point to new ways to think about land and occupation.

We're not just four random people; we're part of a family. The eldest two of us — Matt and Selena — arrived in Vancouver in the summer of 1991, with Selena four months pregnant. Matt's friend Electra let us stay with her while we looked for jobs and a place to live. She lived in a studio apartment above a jewellery store on Commercial Drive, so we stretched out our camping mats under her kitchen table. Matt grew up on Vancouver Island and would come to the city for punk shows when he was a teenager, so he knew that this was the area we wanted to be in. It wasn't quite the Lower East Side of Manhattan, where we'd just been living, but it was the best place we could think of to have a baby.

Coming west was kind of like coming home for Matt, a fourth-generation descendent of English, Irish and French immigrants on the West Coast. However, for Selena (who grew up on Canadian military bases as a sixth-generation descendent of Irish settlers to Prince Edward

Island and an eleventh-generation descendent of French settlers to the lands south of Québec City), Vancouver, and East Vancouver in particular, was almost a foreign country. The money was the same, English was the main language (with hardly any French), and there was a surprising imprinting of Indigenous iconography around the city. It was the summer after the resistance at Kanehsatà:ke and Kahnawá:ke,[1] and we had been involved in Indigenous solidarity work for several years in Ontario — not because we had any deep understanding of decolonization or anything, but because some wonderful and trusted older activist mentors gave us clear directions on how we might use our energies more effectively. Even though we had spent time in and with many Indigenous communities, our notions of solidarity were remarkably unsophisticated and vestigial.

We moved into East Vancouver and began enjoying the privileges of educated, white (if broke) young folks, like the walkable streets, cheap food and the diversity of personal expressions, sexualities and politics that made up the area at the time. We started volunteering for La Quena Coffeehouse, an anti-capitalist organizing space that supported struggles in Latin America, and through that space we made friends. In our limited understanding of Indigenous struggles at the time, we thought that they always occurred outside of cities and in faraway places. We had never heard the phrase "unceded territory." We vaguely knew there were some treaties that had been negotiated (and thereafter broken) for the territories our ancestors lived in, but we didn't know the details of them. Learning how to be a respectful visitor to these lands is a long process, and we are very far from confident in this; neither are we anything like resolved in our thinking. It is a fraught process in which there are no easy conclusions. Thinking hard and critically about our place here and understanding the history of settler development is a central part of it, but not all of it.

During Selena's pregnancy we walked a lot, often past Victoria Park; we were surprised to see the crowds of older men intensely playing bocce ball and gambling. On the first full day of her slowly developing labour, we went out for a walk to speed things along. As had become our habit, we hung out in the park. It was the middle of January 1992 and a surprisingly sunny day. Contractions were fierce, so we walked slowly, around and around the park's one square block. We weren't paying much attention to other people, but we were happy to be out in the sun, and the bocce games were a good distraction from her contraction pains. Sadie was born the next day at 2:00 a.m.

Five years later, in the summer of 1997, we were still living beside the park, but in a different apartment, and now we were going there daily to play. As Selena laboured in a plastic wading pool filled with water in our bedroom to give birth to Daisy, a succession of friends came and took Sadie to play in Bocce Ball Park. And now, two decades later, we live on the far side of the park, where we have rented the same house for twenty years. We still see Bocce Ball Park every day from our kitchen table.

Even though the four of us have different intersections with our place here, we are each curious about occupations in general, and much more pressingly, how our own various occupations of this land can be transformed. East Vancouver in general, and Commercial Drive especially, has historically been an exuberant place, welcoming newcomers from all over the globe: visitors like us, others who have been forcibly brought to these lands and all kinds of people escaping untenable situations. Come to the Drive on a sunny day and you'll see a frothy mix of people mostly able to share land easily and well. And there is maybe no better place to witness it than in Bocce Ball Park, where everyday activities give us clues as to how we can share land in a decolonial sense.

Because of, and despite, all the volatile political and emotional responses parks elicit, we, like most everyone else, have a lot of love for parks. And maybe more than anywhere, we love the little park beside our house. We think that a close examination of this one small patch of grass might produce some generative conversations about land (parks and otherwise) and, more than that, force us to confront our confused and confusing attitudes toward occupation. We're after a renovated politics of land, in the context of our ongoing occupation. This project speaks directly and frankly to settlers[2] like us: how can we disavow the colonial attitudes that stain all our thinking about land? And how can we simultaneously embrace the good, durable and ineffable communities that have formed on these lands?

We have lived in East Vancouver for twenty-seven years now, and we still have a lot of love for this neighbourhood, even as it is buffeted by gentrifications. We have raised a family and grown up here. We feel like we have a certain connection, a fidelity to this place — but our residency is precarious. We're renters, for one, so our tenure is always tenuous. And our love for Commercial Drive is being tested perilously. Frankly, this is a very different place than we signed up for. The neighbourhood has become less diverse, the housing wildly more expensive, the streets a little more generic, the pretentiousness more toxic, the displacements endemic. We presume that our tenure here will not last much longer. We have fought off one renoviction already; the next time we will surely look elsewhere.

But in an even deeper and more critical sense, we are precarious because our presence is predicated on colonial land theft, on illegitimate grounds. We're uninvited visitors on stolen Indigenous territory. And, honestly, we're not really sure what to do about that. We know that almost everything has to change about how we encounter land and that our ways of living need to change — but we are unclear about what that means exactly. This book project is a small reckoning with these truths, an attempt to take on these realities in a local and personal way, by looking closely at the land right here — one small piece of land we see and smell and hear every day.

Victoria Park is just an average, small-ish city park, one you'd easily miss on any map of the area. Few people notice or pay much attention to it unless they live nearby. In a lot of other ways, though, there is so much to talk about in Bocce Ball Park. That one square block articulates so many of the aporias of occupied urban land. So that's what this book is: a close portrait of Bocce Ball Park as a narrative thread and case study, as a route to talking about the occupation of land and especially parks. In talking about Bocce Ball Park, we are trying to think about parks broadly, through specific histories of settlement and treaty, and theorizing about land in all its pluralities.

Perhaps the only remarkable part of Bocce Ball Park is the intense density and diversity of uses: grizzled bocce ball players shouting and gambling, hipsters doing hipster things, dog-walkers, kids of all ages, a Latinx harm-reduction group, parents and caregivers, readers, drinkers,

Victoria Park, day 32. Photo by Daisy Couture

drug users, guitar players, soccer players, youth camps, meetings and people sleeping in the sun and overnight. In most ways though, it is a totally unremarkable park. It's easy to miss, easy to ignore — it's indistinguishable, really, from scores of others just like it in the city. It is just a patch of grass with a gravel path arcing through one side and a fringe of trees lining each edge. There is a playground, a bathroom and two bocce ball runs. Some benches, a water fountain and an arbour-kind-of-thing near the bocce runs. A few modest historical photos are implanted into small boulders along the path. It's just a humble urban park that looks and acts a lot like run-of-the-mill parks in every city.

All parks, and this one in particular, are sites where the exercise of sovereignty — who has authority over specifically defined territories — is unclear and unsteady. People assume that parks are public so they should be allowed to do their thing there, but those things inevitably collide with other people's things. And park regulations. And neighbours. And laws and bylaws. And righteous indignation about what parks *are for*. One of the great virtues of many parks is that, despite all the pretences (and occasional violence) of regulation, they often act as safe zones where people can get away with things they never would be able to, say, on sidewalks or in a library. Parks often emerge as petri dishes for urban experimentation, and Bocce Ball Park is a lively and fecund example. At almost any time of the day or night, someone is pushing against some limits: pitching a tent for overnight camping, slacklining, jumping off the swings for the first time, hosting a party, getting high, laying down a 200 foot slippery slide, hitting a golf ball, drinking, practising tai chi, letting their dog run wild, or making sure everyone knows they are the baddest dude there. And that's almost precisely why we love that park.

But parks are not abstract spatial creations; they are always complicit in and with power. Parks are almost always key players in displacements, and Bocce Ball Park is no different: its energy and audacity are a clear drawing card for realtors and incoming capital, who love to tout the edginess and "urban grit" of our neighbourhood. In cities across the world, but in Vancouver especially, property values and gentrification are numbingly constant topics of discussion, narratives that simultaneously obscure and highlight Indigenous dislocations on the same territory. Older narratives of displacement and dispossession are carried into the twenty-first century with new kinds of claims to property, and those with the most money get to choose where to live while those without are relegated to picking through the leftovers. Bocce Ball Park, like every park, is not exempt from responsibility. Hardly a week goes by without one more jackass realtor unashamedly leaving a vampiric letter in our mailbox hoping to buy this house, always noting that our proximity to Victoria Park is a major draw for eager "pre-approved buyers." The park has to account for its role in the slow destruction of this neighbourhood, just as we all have to account for our roles in settler-colonial dominations.

In all its complicities, duplicities and fraughtness, Bocce Ball Park is also *our* park. We love it and know it intimately, and we like to imagine that it knows and loves us back. The kids have grown up playing on the playgrounds; we traverse it nearly daily and constantly observe it directly and indirectly. We throw baseballs, walk dogs, check on passed-out people, comfort babies, use the toilet in emergencies, smell the pot smokers, and listen to fights and music and old guys yelling at each other in Italian. We've hosted huge potlucks with scores of neighbours, attended meetings and rallies, watched movies, held festivals, attended performances and avoided all kinds of people and events there.

It sometimes gets a little hairy. In the early days it was commonly known as "Man-Down Park" because it is close to the liquor store and there was a consistent tempo of first-responders and ambulances attending to people. No small number of police incidents have occurred over the years, some pretty alarming. There are a lot of folks drifting around at any time of night or day, and the drinking and drug use have always been matters of local contention. Debates about the park's safety are ongoing, especially as it relates to women, especially at night. But despite, or actually because of it all, we overwhelmingly think of Bocce Ball Park as an exemplar of both commonality and difference. Come visit almost any time of day or year and you will see all kinds of people doing all kinds of things in close proximity with remarkably little friction. Like every park, it contains so many stories, so much history, so many relationships; for many people it is among the primary places to experience the city. We want to tell part of the park's story here, to interrogate it as a place, as particular kind of urban subjectivity. But more than that, we want to use it as a vehicle for thinking about occupations, the uses of urban parks, the quasi-spiritual claims for the natural world and the history of this city.

Most importantly, this book is trying to think through relationships with land. We're a white, settler family on Indigenous territory. That reality seeps into every political question, staining all of our legacies. Colonialism both gives settlers permissions and forecloses on us, all in the same breath. Our heritage forces us to confront our genocidal lineages and to ask how we can live on this land with some dignity and respect. It asks how we can eschew simple narratives of reconciliation and contribute to restitution. The urban question is always a question of land, and this land where we live was straight stolen. Now it is occupied — by settlers like us but also by all kinds of other people and other-than-humans who have arrived via every imaginable route and from every corner of the globe.

The book is composed of multiple elements, each informing and entwining with one another, an overlapping assemblage that mimics the dense pluralities of the park. Each element was developed semi-autonomously, with significant formal and informal contributions from all of us, and each element implicitly and explicitly references the others.

Victoria Park, day 88. Photo by Daisy Couture

Daisy documented the park with one photo every day from the exact same spot (the southwest corner) for a year, as well as many other photos. A selection of her photos is distributed throughout the book and serves to both illuminate the space of the park and ground our work in seasonality, everyday-ness and familiarity. The full set of 365 colour images is available online via the Fernwood website (https://fernwoodpublishing. ca/resources/on-this-patch-of-grass). Sadie interviewed a whole range of people who use and think about the park: dog people, kids, drinkers, parents, bocce players, neighbours and more, asking after their ideas, memories, contentions and feelings about the park. These interviews were recorded in text, audio and photographs and are discussed by Sadie, more of which are also available on the website.

Selena wrote an historical and archival examination of the property title to the land on which the park was constructed. She considers how the place that became the park represents and articulates the assumptions of property ownership by settlers in relation to Indigenous peoples' continuing refusal of such colonial constructions. Matt wrote an essay exploring the idea of nature in the city, how ecological discourses around urban parks are mobilized, how they are positioned in urban planning conversations and how parks might contribute to decolonial horizons.

In addition, we asked three people who we admire tremendously and whose work has significantly influenced us in various ways to contribute to the book. All three are friends and interlocutors, as well as critically influential thinkers but from very different backgrounds than us and each other. Denise Ferreira da Silva is a professor and director of the Institute for Gender, Race, Sexuality and Social Justice at the University of British Columbia. Erick Villagomez is a designer, architect, landscape architect, writer, painter and illustrator who teaches at several universities. Glen Coulthard is a member of the Yellowknives Dene First Nation and an associate professor in the First Nations and Indigenous Studies Program and the Department of Political Science at the University of British Columbia. We are grateful and honoured to have all three contribute their thoughts to the book.

Each of these pieces stands alone, and together they represent one interrogation of a small urban park. We hope that this story of Bocce Ball Park will be a fruitful way to think about the roles of parks in the lives of cities, the histories saturating the everyday land all around us and how this knowledge can guide more respectful and responsible relationships in sharing the land.

2

A BETTER
LANDSCAPE

"*Go home* son. We don't want you here. Go back to wherever you are from. This is *our* land, not *yours*. This is *Indian* land. This land is not for white people."

She wasn't being awful but, holy cow, was she ever *direct*. And she was standing right in my way, not letting me pass. I had no idea what to do, so I just stood there and listened as she repeated herself. I tried to interject some quasi-sympathetic comments but realized how stupid I sounded, so I pulled up and just listened. It was a beautiful, summery Saturday morning and I had been crossing the park, wandering through the sunshine, my thoughts drifting easily. There were a bunch of people, mostly older and Indigenous, sitting on a bench just off the path, and I guess she had been in the process of leaving and just ended up crossing my route. Or maybe not. Maybe she had seen me coming and had decided to speak her mind. Maybe she confronted every white person she could. Or maybe I was just someone who she figured needed some talking to.

I stood there for what seemed like a really long time, even though it was probably less than thirty seconds. But it was long enough that someone else, an Indigenous guy I know from around the neighbourhood (at least enough to say hello to) got up off the bench and barked at her to leave me alone. He said that I was okay. A few hipsters had strolled up behind me on the path; there were small clumps of parents in the playground with their kids and a few other people sitting around. Everyone was giving the situation a wide berth, pretending it wasn't happening. It was definitely a little weird and uncomfortable: an older Indigenous woman confronting a much younger white dude in public with overt hostility and intent. I stood there rooted to the spot, stunned. The other guy grabbed her arm and steered her around me. As we passed she deliberately bumped my shoulder and stared right at me. It felt like she was just short of spitting at me. I took a deep breath and kept walking, entirely unsure how to feel. I turned her argument over and over in my head for the rest of the day. What should I have said? The right answer: I should have said nothing, just listened. She was correct: my family and I live on the unceded, traditional and occupied territories of the Musqueam (xʷməθkʷəy̓əm), Squamish (Sḵwx̱wú7mesh) and Tsleil-Waututh (səlilw̓ətaʔɬ) nations. And when I say "occupied," I mean by people like me. By me. She was right — it *is* her land by any measure, ethical or legal.

My kids and I were born here on the west coast of Canada. We've lived in East Vancouver for twenty-five years — that's their whole life. We are *from here,* aren't we? I'm the fourth generation of my family to settle here on Coast Salish land. My heritage is a common kind of waspy mongrel: English, Irish, French, Scottish, probably more. Honestly though, I have no clue how much of any of those things I am, or what kind of heritage I could claim. I have very little connection to or interest in any of those lineages and have never done any kind of family-tree investigations into my ancestry. Really, the only things I know about my forebears are stories my grandmother and parents told me. Stories that I may or may not have straight. It's just never really been of much interest to me.

I am certainly white though: a pasty, blotchy Northern/Western European kind of white. Selena has a similarly hybrid kind of background, much more French (from her dad's side) to my British, and her mom was Scottish/Irish from Prince Edward Island; thus our kids, like us, are just another bunch of mongrels. But we are all unmistakably and unequivocally visible as white, and maybe more accurately, not *from here*, really. There is no way to understand our place here as anything other than colonial. So, maybe we *should* be getting out of here. But that sounds weird to my ears. I think it's better to ask: how can we make sense of the woman's — correct — claim that this is her territory, that this land was stolen?

Thinking through the woman's comments to me — and taking them seriously — seems like one fruitful route to consider decolonization, not in the abstract, not as metaphor, but in the everyday, grounded, landed sense. I agree with her when she says this is her land, not mine. I take

Victoria Park, day 48. Photo by Daisy Couture

that generally, but also specifically (i.e., the park) — but I'm unsure what that might mean next.

These questions cannot and should not be framed as questions of white fragility, anxiety or guilt. That kind of white hand-wringing is profoundly unhelpful and has to be marginalized. Parsing my emotional contours on this point is of little interest to me, let alone anyone else. I do want to ask after the occupation of parks, though, as a route to a renovated politics of land. Parklands are often positioned as apolitical, as "common" or public land that somehow eludes examination amidst the grit of property markets and land-use battles, but it is critical to understand parks as a central feature of colonial land logics, as aggressively regulating and disciplining land and its occupations. Quandamooka Nation scholar Aileen Moreton-Robinson writes:

> It takes a great deal of work to maintain Canada, the United
> States, Hawai'i, New Zealand and Australia as white possessions.
> The regulatory mechanisms of these nation-states are extremely

busy reaffirming and reproducing this possessiveness through a process of perpetual Indigenous dispossession, ranging from the refusal of Indigenous sovereignty to overregulated piecemeal concessions. (2015: xi)

It takes a great deal of work to maintain parks as buttresses of colonial occupation. To interrogate the "park idea," it is necessary to understand how parks have been deployed historically and how they have emerged today. We have to know how Bocce Ball Park came to be and ask what it, and all parks, *want*. We have to ask about its occupations, who has made decisions there, who controls it, who calls it *theirs*. That little park, like all other parks, is not just a random patch of grass. It is being built and rebuilt, bit by bit, day by day, and like all the rest of us, it has to be subjected to a decolonizing gaze. Parks cannot feign innocence, and Bocce Ball Park is not exempt.

That incident with the woman is not the only confrontation I've had in Bocce Ball Park. Actually, that sounds rougher than I mean — I've never had any kind of physically damaging encounter; I've never been jacked or mugged or assaulted. But that doesn't mean it's a delicate place. It's a pretty messy, vibrant and funky spot, and everyone around the park has had to face up to certain kinds of difference and certain kinds of uncomfortableness.

The one rough spot I've ever been in happened in the late 1990s. I was traversing the park diagonally, coming home from the bar on a Friday night. Not late at all, maybe ten-thirty or so. At the far corner there were four or five crusty punk kids who for the past couple of weeks had been camping under the kids' play equipment. But this time they were acting strangely: flailing their arms, swearing and reeling around erratically. I stopped and asked what was up, noticing quickly that at least a couple of them had blood streaming' from their face and head. Another guy was sitting at the bottom of the yellow plastic slide, rocking slowly with his head in his hands and moaning loudly. A young woman was crying and talking profanely about vengeance. They said they had been "overpowered."

I had no idea what they were talking about. There was no one else around and the park was dead quiet. I asked what kind of help I could provide, maybe a drive to the hospital? They declined exuberantly and dismissed me. I paused and thought about it for a moment, waited, then carried on my way, not sure what else to do. It was very dark and I was almost in the exact middle of park when I figured out what had happened. I obviously wasn't very alert, because before I knew what was going on, I found myself surrounded by a circle of seven or eight young men. I didn't know where they had come from or how in the hell I didn't notice them: I was walking across a small field and there was nowhere for them to hide. But it was dark, and I was in my own head, and they surprised me.

I took a quick look around me and immediately realized that they were in front, behind and on all sides. The one in front of me sneered, "Why were you talking to those dudes over there? Are you with them?" I peered through the nighttime murk trying to get a sense of the guy. I answered in the negative, and asked back, "Did you do that to them? Why?" Several laughed: "That was us. We wrecked them. Cause we felt like it." Snickers. I could feel them closing in slightly. I can fight, and actually really like combat sports, but I'm no Bruce Lee and this was only going to go badly, likely extremely badly. Options flashed through my head: there seemed to be a gap between those two guys there, maybe I could bust through and make it home? My front door was only a couple hundred yards away. Maybe that gap wasn't really there though. Maybe I should get a few good shots in on this little prick in front of me? I had pretty much settled on just turtling after the first blow: going down in the dark covering my head and groin and hoping for the best.

It was getting close to showtime. I could instinctually feel it coming and figured the first shot was going to come from behind. So I turned sharply and encountered a minor revelation. It was Vlad. Bad Vlad. For years, I had been running informal basketball games at the school court just down the street. Me and my idiot buddies would gather every Saturday morning for a hung-over run of basketball, and over time, a pack of kids — teenagers and younger — would join us. It was always a good run, eventually degenerating into a huge free-for-all, but some of the more talented kids got pretty good, and we had some skilled games. One of those kids was Bad Vlad.

I hadn't seen him for some years. He was probably thirteen or fourteen back then: a tall, quiet kid, who had some ball skills and didn't speak English all that well. He'd always been friendly and polite, but I didn't know much about him, or really about most of those kids. I worked at keeping their names straight, but didn't have connection with them beyond those Saturday mornings. I saw some of the kids occasionally around the neighbourhood and did know that a few of them had graduated into the drug trade. Most of them were minor hustlers, but once I had seen one of them (a guy that I did know well) sprinting down a busy sidewalk in a full-on panic. He had crossed the wrong gangsters and ended up spending a few nights locked naked in the trunk of a car in a mall parking lot before the cops fished him out.

I guess Vlad had tended in that direction as well, and that evening I had never been so glad to see him. Actually, rarely have I been that glad to see *anyone*. I yelped "*Hey! Vlad!* It's me. *Matt!*" It felt like the whole circle of us took a collective intake of breath and paused. Vlad and I looked at each other for a pregnant moment, and then all the tension released as he acknowledged me, grasped my outstretched hand and bro-hugged me. I held him for a half-second and as he smiled hugely, "*You're lucky it's me, huh?*" No fucking kidding. *No fucking kidding.* The circle sort of dissipated and melted away, and I continued on my way, all rubber-legged, got home and locked the door behind me.

That was it. That's really the only time I felt in danger in the park or its environs, although for years afterwards I avoided walking across the middle of it any time after dark. Some say "a conservative is a liberal who has been mugged," but that situation didn't change my views of community safety and security much, if at all. In some ways, it concretized them. I still think that parks are inherently safety-generating spaces: the more people who are in public, the more unscheduled interactions we have with our neighbours, the more we see each other, the safer we all are. This is classic urban theory, Jacobsian "eyes on the street," a shared visibility that securitizes seamlessly, the antipode to all of us cowering behind locked doors, video cameras, guards, alarmed security systems, Fox News and burgeoning paranoia. Parks, in their very construction, support collective safety.

Victoria Park, day 103. Photo by Daisy Couture

But that's not always right. For many, parks represent lurking danger, full of unpredictability. Think of the Central Park rapist, the Stanley Park "Babes in the Wood" killings, all the stories you have heard of sexual assaults or muggings in parks, all the times you have heard of the bodies of murder victims being found in parks. Or all the tiresomely pedestrian, smaller acts of harassment or irritation or violation you have heard of or encountered. I always hope Selena, the kids and really everyone, think twice about crossing Bocce Ball Park, or most any park, at night. Parks, like every urban space, are socially manufactured and we all experience them differently. For some of us, parks are mostly to be avoided and are patently dangerous spots.

Bocce Ball Park isn't that kind of place, I don't think. I'm afraid I am giving a wrong impression by telling these two stories up front. It's a peaceable spot. It's kind of amazing actually. There are all kinds of people who use the park in all kinds of ways. There is a fantastic density and diversity of users, and we all get along almost all of the time. There are bocce ball players and card-playing gamblers, street types, plenty of drinking and drugging, middle-class kids and families, hipsters, dog people and dogs, punks, homeless people, rowdy teenagers, nerds reading books, sunbathers and tons else. And without much overt regulation or monitoring, it all works out beautifully, almost all the time.

At least that was what I was arguing at a community meeting a few years back. Actually, it wasn't a "community" meeting at all — it was a gathering of local homeowners who were claiming they were "concerned" about the park and wanted to do "something" about it. What they really meant was they wanted the park "cleaned up" of the rabble. It was an unadorned class maneuver. You know these types: there are renditions of these working in every neighbourhood in every city everywhere. They claim "their" park is being overrun by homeless people, addicts, whoever — and call for more police interventions, security cameras and so on. In this case, they were making a big push for the city to install weird blue lights throughout the park that supposedly make it impossible for intravenous drug-users to find their veins.

I was not invited to this meeting. I am a renter and my political positions are well-known. I am not welcome among these people, but a sympathetic neighbour let me know about the (small) event so I invited myself. It was supposed to be a meeting of concerned neighbours to talk about issues regarding the park and I seemed to qualify (and figured there might be expensive snacks) so I went. I listened semi-patiently as one person after the other complained about the Indigenous kids and the older Latinx guys who gather there to drink daily, about the homeless and punk rock campers, about the garbage and noise. When it was my turn, I was fuming and gave a righteously energetic speech extolling the virtues of the park, of all the difference it contained, of how proud I was of how many people the park welcomed.

A smaller, older Asian woman waited until I finished. She looked right at me and quietly said: "You don't mind crossing the park because those men don't yell awful things at you." I paused and took a breath, agreed with her and, chastened, sat down. And of course she was right. I'm a healthy, middle-aged, white dude who goes to the gym. I rarely feel physically threatened in the park. When I got home I asked the women in my house if that was their experience too. "Do those guys yell shit at you?" Sadie said, "Yeah of course they do. So often." She said she just ignored them, but it was irritating. I had no idea.

Which was (yet another) stark reminder of intersectionality. The park does contain multitudes and that's wonderful, but each of us encounters each one of those elements, individually and in endless combinations, differently. And as a relatively well-off settler I am oblivious to most of them. What I see as contested, messy and vibrant is felt as terrifying by some. If I tilt my head in one direction, I can totally see what they are talking about. There are very often people passed out in the grass, cops show up frequently, there is a lot of substance abuse, there are occasionally people looking for scraps, it is noisy and dirty sometimes. But look the other way and there's something else going on, something that I think is critical to city life.

In many discourses, parks are posited as the best of urbanity, as an unmitigated "good" that represents all that cities can and should be. Parks are purportedly natural salves for the disordered immorality and filth of urban life, pools of respite, beauty and virtue. But those complicated and complicating claims make multiple contradictory and dubious arguments for human social and political life that are not easily dislodged or disentangled. Those claims are always bound up with rationalities of whiteness and colonial ordering: parks bring structured comprehensibility and access to the otherwise unruly "wilds," cleansed of any savage and uncooperative residents, and disallow any activities that do not adhere to certain orders. A huge amount of work is expended on park design to ensure that they adhere *exactly* to settler colonial re-orderings of occupation. To untangle these logics is it critical to understand a little about the emergence of the "park idea" in North America and to know a little of the genealogy of Bocce Ball Park.

The history of the urban parks movement in Europe and North America closely tracks and is intimately bound up with the history of contemporary urban planning. The best starting point for this narrative is the Industrial Revolution, which transformed essentially everything that anyone had ever understood about cities. From the late 1700s and throughout the 1800s, urban landscapes were radically restructured in the image of factories. Waves upon waves of workers and their families flooded into Western cities, industrial production dominated civic agendas both political and material, and every aspect of social life — from the provision of services, the allocation of wages, notions of citizenship and the invention of modern recreation — was transformed as cities were remade as and by mass-scaled manufacturing units.

The early epochs of industrialization were profoundly transformative for city residents as every semblance of existing order was thrown into contention. Craft workers, mercantilist classes, state actors, bourgeoisie and aristocrats alike saw their spheres of influence, their revenue streams, their expectations of production and consumption, their patterns of living all disrupted with catastrophic speed, but of course and as always, it was poor inhabitants who were most deleteriously affected. The Victorian city, the City of the Dreadful Night, is fabled in literature and historical imaginarias for Dickensian squalor, spectacular overcrowding and ill-sanitation, for grotesque pollution, for poverty and deprivation, for vice and moral decrepitude. There are certainly elements of truth to these narratives of nineteenth-century cities out of control, and in all ways, the early industrial city was disconcerting and dismaying. The Industrial Revolution upset every kind of urban order, turned over every certainty of commerce and construction, and cast into doubt the safety, hygiene and even viability of cities themselves.

Urban elites inserted themselves with force into this roiling mess. Gathering up their shock and awe, throughout the 1800s dominant classes of the city asserted and reasserted the need for a reconstituted order that could reconcile class dominance in the new context. Civic reform efforts, temperance movements and religious retrenchments jostled with the first applications of zoning laws, mass-scale sewage and municipal sanitation efforts, building permits and building codes, new policing mandates and engineering exercises, new state intrusions and ordering. In every city, authorities and elites deployed multiple strategies on multiple fronts over the course of decades, furiously trying to reassert authority and order, to bring the city back under control and maybe more than anything, to suppress the incipient threats of insurrection.

The industrial city was full of workers and lower classes cramped together, often in disastrous housing and social milieus, bound by the poverty wages of the new factories. The conditions were perfect for fomenting civil unrest, socialist and anarchist organizing, insurrectionary theorizing and generalized social instability: a circumstance hardly lost on dominant classes in industrial cities across Europe, America and colonized cities around the world. The fear of riot and rebellion was at the heart of the invention of civic and urban planning, of trying to bring order to the unruly crowds, of pacifying the masses, of preventing wholesale revolution.

The rise of urban planning through the 1800s rested on narratives closely correlating environmental pollution and filth with moral decline and depravity, and thus with political instability. Civic reformers argued repeatedly that unsanitary living and working conditions would nurture aberrant personal and social immoralities, which would then easily give permission to political revolutions. The answers to the unstable, polluted and potentially dangerous powder kegs of cities should thus be found in the re-creation of physical order, of urban civility, of architectural and planning pacifications. Parks were always — and remain — a central tactical feature of these campaigns.

If the city was the problem — filthy, polluted, cramped, disordered, unpredictable, immoral, sexualized, depraved and licentious — then the natural world was the antidote. To the burgeoning romanticized minds of nineteenth-century civic reformers and elites, "nature" was everything that cities were not: virginal, ordered, peaceful, beatific, full of open vistas, breathable air, clear thinking and virtuous, pure ideals. If the city was out of control, the natural world could calm and re-order it.

To most Eurospheric planners of the time, the Platonic ideal of a park was the Gardens of Versailles, or for those with more Orientalist/colonial bents, the Taj Mahal grounds. These monumental exercises represented a kind of apogee of human-natural engagement: perfectly ordered and structurally magnificent, but also serene and uplifting with resplendent gardens and foliage, perfect paths leading to leaping fountains and contemplative pools, and open, clean and sensorially grounding aesthetics all around.

This particular Euro-tradition of densely structured, rationally planned natural features inserted into highly formalized urban environments inspired generations of planners, architects and designers. Perhaps the most fulsomely built expressions of these sensibilities in North America were articulated by the City Beautiful movement and driven by visionaries like Daniel Burnham and Emmanuel Louis Masqueray, who argued powerfully for the remaking of civic order and virtue via highly structured monumental beatification. The largest-scale effects of City Beautiful planning can be seen most obviously in places like the waterfront of Chicago, the Washington Mall and the core of Memphis, Tennessee, but more modest expression can be found in parks, promenades, gardens and all kinds of parkesque spaces in cities across the globe. Burnham is best remembered for his "Make no small plans" exhortation, but a better evocation of his urban influence is: "Let your watchword be order and your beacon beauty."

But there is another primary strain in Western urban park building that is equally powerful and resonant, one that stems from congruent intellectual presumptions and beliefs, but takes a different tack in terms of both design and intention. While the formalized City Beautiful movement and all its neo-classical and beaux arts antecedents took a monumental approach that gestured towards authoritarian and class-calcified social orders, Frederick Law Olmsted brought a wholly divergent set of philosophical and design orientations to park design.

Olmsted was a well-known American journalist and social critic who became intrigued by the English garden tradition after a trip to Europe. In 1858 he and his architectural partner Calvert Vaux won the competition to design New York's Central Park, which required the removal of Seneca Village, a primarily African-American community (as well as some Irish and German immigrants) that included about 20 percent of New York's property-owning (and thus eligible to vote) Blacks. And of course all of what would become Central Park was Indigenous land that had been long cleared.

Olmsted's vision for the park took much of its inspiration from the progressive movement and democratic ideals (without paying too much thought, of course, to the vast displacement required to lay the table for this vision), explicitly referencing a social order counter-posed to the densely geometric formal regimentations of European palace-parks and City Beautiful landscapes. He imagined a park where working people could assemble after a hard day's labour, where poor children could roam freely and where multiplicities of recreational opportunities abounded.

Shot throughout Olmstedian philosophy is a deep-seated and extroverted anti-urbanism. The egalitarian tendencies in his thinking consistently reference the idea of the park as an "outlet" for working class and poor city residents, who without access to recreational opportunities might use their leisure time to become disillusioned and disruptive. He designed parks to "counteract the evils of town life," and unlike the restricted and restricting constructions of continental Europe, his designs were naturalistic, pastoral and picturesque. His parks were carefully ordered and structured to appear as disordered and unstructured as possible. He sought curving pathways, water features that appeared unexpectedly and organic spaces that fluidly merged with one another, and he made every effort to mimic the natural world and to "conceal the hand of man." He eschewed straight lines and right angles, constantly seeking to produce smooth irregularities and picturesque arrangements of small lakes, rocky outcroppings, trees, shrubs, broken terrains, ravines and glades, meadows and creeks.

Olmsted's influence on North American park design and landscape architecture can hardly be overstated. Central Park in Manhattan and Prospect Park in Brooklyn are probably his two most famous creations, but he and Vaux built a mind-boggling number of major parks and park systems in cities across the continent: Mount Royal in Montreal, the White House and Capitol grounds in Washington DC, Boston's Emerald Necklace, the entire parks and parkway system of Louisville, the Grand Necklace of parks in Milwaukee, and many more. As well, he designed scores of academic campuses from Yale to Stanford to Berkeley to Chicago, and had a significant role in the early conservation movement, including considerable efforts to preserve Niagara Falls, Yosemite and the Adirondacks and to create the national parks system. Innumerable landscape architects and designers since have carried his legacy forward, most notably his two sons, who worked as the Olmsted Brothers right up until 1950. The strong likelihood is that you have spent considerable time in one of his creations.

Olmsted and Vaux were hardly the only park designers operating in North America through the late-1800s but they were by far the most successful in articulating the picturesque ideal of how a park should operate and what it should do. In an era of Thoreau and Wordsworth, Friedrich and Emerson, Keats and Fichte, Olmstedian park theory resonated acutely with the romantic and transcendentalist movements. The anti-modernist romantics powerfully decried the brutality, immoralities and pollution of industrial cities while reifying the "natural" as authentic, restorative, purely moral and clean. Parks were to improve both the city and its inhabitants, but also to transcend it, to be all the city was not.

The Olmstedian oeuvre and the century-plus of subsequent park movements that draw from the same theoretical wells are beset with ironies from all sides. The picturesque park requires intense levels of human intervention to create and maintain particular aesthetic sensibilities. The "authentic" landscapes of Olmsted's parks are manufactured with expert precision by teams of engineers, labourers, landscape architects, gardeners, bureaucrats and many more. His oft-repeated dictum to "conceal the hand of man" requires huge amounts of human skill, artistry and persistence to manage visages of authenticity. What the Olmstedian park claims as "natural" barely adheres to even the most elastic popular definitions of the term. And all his "naturalist" impulses require a terra nullius cleansing of the landscapes, vast displacements and dispossessions, and continual strict policing and regulation to freeze the picture in place.

These two dominant strains of thinking about urban parks from the 1800s — the highly formalized, geometric and structured European garden traditions, and their design antipode, the Olmstedian naturalistic, romanticized and picturesque parks — are often counter-posed to one another by historians, and rightly so. The former tended to elitist, even authoritarian, monumental thinking about cities, while the latter evinced an anti-urban populism fueled by American democratic impulses. It is true that these two traditions represent divergent ideals of what parks could and should be for, but both survive energetically in contemporary park thinking, each working and winding through landscape architecture, park design and building practices.

However, these easy dualistic narratives substantially miss what both traditions share: an abiding interest in the assertion of order, pacifying the unruly city, instrumentally deploying the natural world for political ends and managing carefully structured renditions of what constitutes

Victoria Park, day 171. Photo by Daisy Couture

appropriate human behaviour. Each park-building tradition deeply invests in enforcing and re-enforcing colonial architectures. Both traditions employ parks and park theory as highly politicized, legislated arenas for city-shaping, for describing social-natural relations and for ordering the good urban subject: white, property-owning, productively employed, happily recreating and passively pacified.

Throughout the twentieth century, these two planning traditions reverberated, entangled, and articulated themselves though currents and countercurrents, new movements and side-eddies of park theory and practice, and both have carried easily into contemporary park building. Reform and recreation agendas have jostled with arguments about safety; claims that parks should be for passive contemplation have butted heads with more active leisure programs; populist agendas have run into proponents of order; and all of it vibrates with historicized arguments about what parks are good for. Working through this project, I kept asking those questions about Bocce Ball Park, and about parks in general:

what should a park be doing? How does Bocce Ball Park structure and reinforce certain kinds of occupation? How might parks, and that park, re-order and create counter-narratives to colonial occupations?

In most contemporary urban writing, Olmsted is venerated in park, planning and urbanist circles for some very good reasons: his popularism, his democratic rationales, the organic feel of his parks, their multiplicity of uses, and their very ubiquity. Pretty much anyone can find an Olmstedian park, or at least an Olmsted-inspired park, close by, and in many ways his picturesque ideals define, limit and infuse what most of us think today about how a good urban park should act. But there are some critical limits in his work, and his foundational narratives have distorted and confined our thinking about the possibility of parks in some highly regrettable ways.

At heart, conventional urban theory rests on the presumption that parks are the best parts of cities, that they are a social good that rectifies the city's ills, that parks can be what cities cannot, and that parks offer respite and meet the inherently unfulfilled needs of urban citizens. Jane Jacobs famously turned that equation on its head in *The Death and Life of Great American Cities* and claimed that it was *parks* that were the problem and that *cities* could fix them. Jacobs ferociously decried any tendencies she perceived as anti-urban, from expressways to garden cities, and in many (maybe even most) parks she saw a long history of Olmstedesque antipathy toward city life materialized. She saw parks all too often turned into dead spaces, devoid of life and energy, stuck in tediously uniform expectations, isolated from the verve and vitality around them. Jacobs' antidote was to infect parks with urbanity: "Let us turn this thought around and consider city parks deprived places that need the boon of life and appreciation conferred on *them* … liveliness and variety attract more liveliness; deadness and monotony repel life" (1961: 89, 106). Throughout her work, Jacobs fetishized a particular and depoliticized rendition of "diversity," and on this point, she has had tremendous impact on contemporary park thinking. Under her gaze, generations of progressive urban planners over the past fifty years have repositioned parks as sites of diverse uses by diverse people. Consider the Vancouver Board of Parks and Recreation's mission statement claiming that it "preserves and advocates for parks and recreation services to benefit all."

I'll get back to that (absurd) claim in a minute, but my point is not whether Jacobs' approach is a better way to think about parks, but to note that she pivoted the conversation about urban parks in three important ways. First, her relentless valourizing of the city is particularly useful in the context of three centuries of anti-urbanist tripe about parks as the antidote to city depredations. Second, she saw density as an ecological imperative, claiming that it is suburban sprawl and low-density development, not cities, that squander energy and resources. And third, she insisted that we look closely at what specific parks do and how they act, rather than retreat into abstracted dogma. What Jacobs missed, and progressive contemporary urban planning exuberantly denies, is any real analysis of occupation, and certainly she had no interest in decolonial analyses of land. Neither Jacobs nor her acolytes care for thinking past the most facile evocations of "diversity" and asking on what grounds parkland was acquired, what colonial histories of displacement those lands contain and what a ritualistic invoking of "diversity" forces out, forgets and dispossesses.

When we talk about any particular park, or city parks in general, what we are really talking about is how urban space could and should be allocated and used. Entwined within those conversations are presumptions about how human relationships with the other-than-human world can and should be mediated and controlled. The notion that parks are "good for people," whether they are immense national parks far from cities or small urban parks set amidst dense residential, commercial and industrial activity, rests on highly questionable ideologies that tend to obscure far more than they illuminate. Claims to "diversity" habitually feign a commitment to commonality without asking after the rationalities that structure the subjects of those commons: who is allowed in and under what conditions?

All arguments regarding human intersections with the other-than-human world are claims for the ordering of particular relationships, that is, their rationale, construction, maintenance, supervision, cataloguing and enforcement. This is the everyday work of biopolitics: the shaping of bodies by people, the conduct of conduct. Park theory is just another set of discourses describing how people should behave, what kinds of activities are tolerable, which are unacceptable, which are encouraged and which punished. For example, Olmsted's pastoral parks love the idea of an English gentleman rambling on a Sunday afternoon and hate the idea of vices like drinking and gambling, just to choose a couple of "goods" and "ills" among many others he delineated.

Running throughout Olmstedian theory is a persistent and insistent return to the "sanitary" functions of parks. He meant this partially in the public health sense, but more so in his belief that access to the pastoral was salutary for individual mental, spiritual and physical well-being — that it is cleansing, purifying and fortifying. All his landscape architecture was planned to produce a whole-mind-and-body effect. For him, the purpose of parks is always to be in service to human needs: "Service must precede art, since all turf, trees, flowers, fences, walks, water, paint, plaster, posts and pillars in or under which there is not a purpose of direct utility or service are inartistic if not barbarous" (quoted in Beveridge 2000). This is about as clear a performance of whiteness as one can imagine. As W.E.B. Du Bois (1920) put it: "I am given to understand that whiteness is the ownership of the earth forever and ever, Amen!"

This has always been the drive behind park movements: improving "nature" and facilitating the consumption and control of more and more of the other-than-human world. Park advocates consistently deploy different kinds of intellectual conventions, but parks are always designed to make the whole world better and more available to human consumptions, or as Olmsted put it, to provide people with "greater enjoyment of scenery than they could otherwise have consistently with convenience within a given space" (quoted in Beveridge 2000). This point is important to reconcile with urban theory, because then we can speak of parks as intensely political matters riddled with questions of territory, jurisdiction and sovereignty.

Parks regularly invoke strong and emotional debates in cities. They are often the loci for people's irritations with the complexities of urban life but also frequently proxies for other kinds of contentions. Conversations about parks, and certainly small neighbourhood parks like Bocce Ball Park, tend to evoke pissed-off opinions, often rendered in jumbled mishmashes of conflicting and conflated arguments, but more often than not, people articulate sophisticated assertions for and about the city. In any conversations about parks, there are a number of questions that need to be asked, but there are three that should be explicitly surfaced, especially when they are obscured behind schlocky dogma like parks should provide "services to benefit all." Obviously, no park, or park system, can "benefit all," and political choices need to be made about who gets to use parks and for what kinds of activities.

Maybe the best question to start with is: *Who gets to speak for parks, and on what grounds?* Many constituencies instinctively presume that they should have the hammer when it comes to park spaces: adjacent homeowners, neighbourhood groups, professional designers, municipal bureaucrats, city planners, developers, police and park users, just to name a few. Then there are the sub-constituencies within those populations. Take, say, "park users" and then think about how often parents of toddlers, dog-people, teenagers, drinkers and ball players clash over even the most nondescript pieces of territory. On every piece of land, there are layers upon layers of authority claimed, and competing and collaborating uses are worked out in a variety of shifting ways.

Consider this example regarding Vancouver's Stanley Park. In 2014 a proposal was made by the Aeriosa and Spakwus Slulem dance groups to perform a collaborative piece at the site of xʷməθkʷəy̓əm, a Coast Salish village that had been in place previous to the creation of Stanley Park. The former is a non-Indigenous group, the latter a Squamish dance troupe, and they proposed performing an innovative dance piece within the park called *The Trees Are Portals*, which would be a remounting of a previous performance called *Thunderbird*. The collaboration was carefully designed and built over the course of years and demonstrated what Tsimshian art historian and dance scholar Dr. Mique'l Dangeli calls "a host/guest relationscape" of considerable complexity (2015: 156). In the process of sorting out the necessary permits and approvals, it was brought to the troupes' attention that the Parks Board perceived an administrative conflict. Part of the performance was to include a paddle song, which administrators believed was potentially a Squamish land claim, which would conflict with the Musqueam and Tsleil-Waututh Nations' claims to the park. As Dangeli writes, there was reason for park officials to inquire, but their approach and understandings of protocol were uninformed:

The assessment that Spakwus Slulem's performance of their canoe song is a land claim is more than justifiable, it is factual, but who has the right to stop that claim from being made? … Northwest Coast First Nations songs, dances and their histories are not only integrally connected to the territories but they are also declaration of hereditary rights to ownership of land and waterways. Paddle songs, in particular, are sung in relation to the people they are addressing.

While paddle songs act as statements by the singers of where they are from, the same songs are also used to respectfully situate dance groups, canoe families, and Nations within territories that do not belong to them. It is not as though the lyrics to the Spakwus Slulem's canoe song deny Musqueam and Tsleil-Waututh claims; rather they situate the singers in relation to Squamish territory and in this case, to their history at Xʷway Xʷway. Simply stated, it is not an exclusive claim but is most certainly a relational one. (188–90)

The Park staff struggled to handle the situation with respect and agility. Earlier that year the City of Vancouver had passed a resolution acknowledging the city as residing on Coast Salish territory and stating that they would be seeking to develop proper protocols for shared uses. Faced with the Aeriosa and Spakwus Slulem's proposal, City and Park staff balked at the possibility that the performance could be interpreted as the Squamish claiming exclusive sovereignty, and in response they required that the troupes obtain written permission from "intergovernmental organizations" (meaning band councils) of the Musqueam and Tseil-Waututh. The Spakwus Slulem troupe explained that the bureaucrats misunderstood Indigenous protocols and how cultural activities were allowed to proceed, and that the responsibility for obtaining permissions was rooted in much older and deeper protocols and processes than settlers were aware of.

The entire scenario became confused, with multiple state actors piling in, and the ironies accumulated with (primarily) one white settler administrator woman and a series of bureaucracies denying Indigenous performers access and imposing protocol in the name of "defending"

Stanley Park. The fact that what is now Stanley Park was brutally cleared of Indigenous inhabitants by colonial authorities to make room for set-tler recreation surely did not escape the administrators, but it failed to dislodge their glacial year-long decision-making process, which did, after much processing and many delays, result in the performance eventually being given the parks board permit.

That particular situation was problematic enough, but it is emblematic of much larger and more entrenched questions and conflicts around who speaks for parks, who speaks for land. The claim that parks should be accessible to "all" is a performatively liberal stance, one that undercuts any agonistic claims and becomes atheoretical and depolitical in the hands of state bureaucracies. All land is saturated with stories and histories, much of it beautiful and honourable, and some awful and violent. Claiming land to be "common" or to be commonly held does not wipe history clean. We live among the accumulating ruins of colonial rationalities, and stating that parks should "benefit all" willfully ignores history and obscures the highly political choices that are being made all around us. Any claim that parks are "open to all" is a naked lie — a lie that is designed to buttress colonial rationalities.

Wrapped up with that first critical question is the second: *Who gets to use parks, and for what purposes?* Olmsted, and much of the early parks movement, had clearly articulated (if patronizing) democratic principles at heart: "All classes represented, with a common purpose, not at all intellectual, competitive with none … You may thus often see vast numbers of persons brought closely together, poor and rich, young and old, Jew and Gentile" (quoted in Twombley 2010: 32). Like most advocates, Olmsted argued that parks should be melting pots, designed for the mingling of classes and ages, a milieu where marginalized people could gather and be soothed and placated. That tradition has always been closely sutured to the idea of *uplift*, that parks have special value for the degraded classes of society, that the very experience of parks should act as a kind of fantastical naturalistic penance, both social and individual.

> No one who has closely observed the conduct of the people who visit the Park, can doubt that it exercises a distinctly harmoniz-ing and refining influence upon the most unfortunate and most

lawless classes of the city — an influence favourable to courtesy, self-control and temperance. (quoted in Twombley 2010: 246)

While the parks movement has always evinced a commitment to the *public*, fidelities to particular kinds of order govern that commitment. It is worth asking what kinds of activities are deemed acceptable in parks, and why? Alcohol consumption is a theme throughout the history of park design (and in our research and interviews showed up with metronomic regularity): Should drinking be permitted (as many jurisdictions around the world allow)? Where? Should private establishments sell alcohol in parks? The selling of food is sometimes allowed in some parks, but soup kitchens and food give-aways are actively disallowed in Vancouver. What about other kinds of commercial activity? How about community organizing? Or events? Most parks, and certainly parks in Vancouver, exhibit deep confusion on these issues.

In most urban parks, there are clearly defined limits, and Vancouver's parks have their own configurations of activities. Most urban parks encourage walking, ball games, reading, contemplative activity and children playing. But not hunting or fishing. Low-incomed people are welcome if they are orderly, but not if they want to sleep overnight, and certainly no multi-night campers. Smoking is prohibited in all parks. Some commercial establishments may be allowed in parks, especially if they generate revenue for the Parks Board, but not poor people selling stuff. Bird watching is okay, but not Indigenous people gathering medicines. Friends of ours were severely rebuked for gathering herbs and plants on their traditional territory because the Parks Board has a strict prohibition on harvesting anything in any park if it is for "personal use."

Dogs are highly contentious. They are conditionally okay in some parks in Vancouver, but only on leashes, or in contained, prescribed circumstances. Other kinds of animals are welcomed: most birds, some insects, some mammals and the occasional raccoons are permitted. Cougars, skunks, bears, rats, otters, crows and coyotes — not so much.[1] The City of Vancouver Parks and Recreation (2018) defines wildlife

as all amphibians, reptiles, birds, and mammals that are native to the province ... Animal species that are found in BC but are not

Victoria Park, day 261. Photo by Daisy Couture

native to the province are not considered wildlife. This includes Common rock doves (pigeons), European starlings, mute swans, and peacocks, rabbits, rats and Eastern grey squirrels. These species are not protected by legislation. If they are a nuisance, they may be dealt with by private pest control companies in a humane manner.

Similarly, certain kinds of plants are encouraged — grass is good, and bushes, shrubbery and managed trees are nurtured. But many other kinds of plants are actively discouraged, severely limited or killed off. What makes the cut or doesn't certainly does not adhere to the "native" condition that (capriciously) applies to animals. Vegetable gardening is rarely welcomed. Ornamental flower gardening is celebrated however. Edible wild foods are not allowed. Nor are brambles, stinging nettles, knotweed or hemp. And certainly, all vegetation has to be kept tidy at all times. Fallen trees, overgrown paths, untended vines, undergrowth gone wild, weeds gone to seed, patchy grass — those rarely find places in parks.

I'm not making an argument here for particular kinds of people, or certain activities, or any kinds of plant or animal; I'm just noting that these are always political choices. The kinds of people, behaviour, plants and animals that are permitted are not "natural" in any sense: they are social decisions, made for particular, and often strangely contradictory, reasons. Why is the privileging of native animal species over recently arrived animals not extended to humans? If animal species that are "found in BC but are not native to the province are *not* considered wildlife [and] not protected by legislation" can be removed and dealt with in a "humane manner" — why are human settlers not removed and dealt with similarly?

This brings us to the third essential question: *What are parks, and Bocce Ball Park in particular, for?* Developers and politicians have always been interested in the ability of parks to lift adjacent land values. Planners love how parks can both limit and enable urban growth patterns. All parks, but especially destination parks, have significant touristic value. Urban reformers have long claimed that parks improve moral, mental and physical health. Social planners and designers love the idea of pacification and refinement of urban populations. And all of these motives tend to rely on Lockean narratives of *improvement*: parks will improve us, improve the other-than-human-world, improve the city and vastly improve upon the previous Indigenous occupations of the land.

There is a close and entangled relationship between who decides for parks, who is permitted to use parks and what parks are for. These three questions need to be woven into every park debate, implicitly and explicitly. Every park employs shifting definitions and deployments of these questions, but typically they are aggressively depoliticized and de-historicized. Certain kinds of histories get remembered and others forgotten; certain practices are beloved, others reviled.

The way these sovereignties and jurisdictions and decisions get played out is often confounding but also often fluid. There's a great sign in Bocce Ball Park that I pass by almost daily. It has some highly prescribed dog rules that include demanding all dogs be kept 15 metres away from the playground. Underneath, on a separate sign, are warnings that to avoid strangulation, people using the play equipment are forbidden to wear helmets, necklaces or clothing with hoods, drawstrings or cords. These strange admonitions are in addition to the 47 pages of "Park Bylaws" that were adopted in 2010 and, of course, apply to Bocce Ball Park. A quick perusal of the bylaw document uncovers gems like the following:

> General Regulations, Article 3(a): No person shall climb, walk, or sit upon any wall, fence or other structure, except play apparatus or seating specifically provided for such use, in or upon any park; or cross, travel on or use any grass plot or land where signs have been posted forbidding such use …
>
> No person shall play at any game whatsoever in or on any portion of any park except upon or in such portions thereof as may be especially allotted, designed and provided, respectively, for any purpose, and under such rules and regulations and at such times as shall be prescribed by the Board …
>
> Article 8(a): No person shall take part in any procession, drill, march, performance, ceremony, concert, gathering or meeting in or on any park or driveway unless with the written permission of the General Manager first had and obtained. (b) No person shall make a public address or demonstration or do any other thing likely to cause a public gathering or attract public attention in any park without the written permission of the General Manager first had and obtained …
>
> Article 8(g): No person shall sing, play a musical instrument, or otherwise perform or provide entertainment in any area of a park which has been designated by the General Manager as an area in which entertainment is not allowed …

Article 16: No person shall play any game or sport in or on any park or recreational facility unless suitably clad and equipped with the requisite appliances for such games, and only at such times, or during the seasons and under such rules and regulations as shall be prescribed by the General Manager.

A quick review: no playing, no sitting, no singing, no music, no sports, no games, no walking, no ceremonies, no meeting, no gathering — except under specific rules and regulations that are determined by the General Manager. This list does not even cite the prohibitions and prescriptions for dogs, fires, cooking, swimming or any other of a thousand kinds of activities that are limited, described, constrained and defined.

I know I'm citing a legal document — and they always sound exceedingly dorky — but these are real prohibitions and regulations that get applied differentially and asymmetrically in real life. Homeless people are ejected from sleeping in parks, people are thrown out for playing the wrong games in the wrong spaces, Indigenous people are prohibited from using ceremonial locations, dance performances are denied permits. And at more subtly biopolitical levels, power is exerted and operationalized at the micro, day-to-day levels via fines, signs, bylaw officers, police, neighbours, regulations, containment and prescription.

One of the reasons we are so fond of Bocce Ball Park is that more than most places, the application and currents of power are openly fluid and negotiable. Right behind that idiotic sign there are typically sizable groups of people openly smoking cigarettes and pot, drinking and gambling while dogs are running free and all kinds of people are wearing hoodies and "clothing with cords and drawstrings." Walk into Bocce Ball Park at any time of night or day and you will immediately witness any number of laws and bylaws being compromised, in any number of ways. The ongoing disobediences in the park — and in almost all parks — are promising: they gesture towards larger possible refusals and re-orderings in hopeful ways.

It's not like Bocce Ball Park is a free-for-all. There is a pretty consistent police presence, especially in the summer, Parks Board workers roll through often, neighbours complain, and the general vibe is regulated by the clear spatial delineation of users: dogs over *there*, bocce *there*, kids basically stay in the playground, drinkers on *those* benches, dope smokers under *those* trees. But part of what I admire so much is the visibility in Bocce Ball Park. The politicization of the park and all the refusals are right there, unmistakable, irreverent. Rather than pacifying the city, this park highlights and amplifies it.

It's not all sunshine, rainbows and unicorns by any stretch. The park still isn't all that comfortable sometimes for a lot of women. Some neighbours feel like they are not really welcome there. Other neighbours don't make it welcome for others. It is a little sketchy sometimes; it's not all that clean, and the grass is patchy, holed and a menace to run across.

There's a lot of dog shit around. There are pockets of hostile yuppies. Police and private security types still harass people regularly. Indigenous people are disallowed from performing ceremonies without permits. But all the ordering being constantly enacted in the park is visible, participatory and unstable. There are so many layers, so many overlapping actors and so much fluidity that it feels in many ways like a place where the competition for urban space has been turned into something closer to a collaborative exercise, or at least one where we can witness power working, and disobey it if necessary.

~

Lastly, I want to poke at the mostly unadorned suggestion that parks are where "nature" happens in the city, and because "nature" is "good for people," parks therefore must be invaluable. That's the basic formulation forwarded time and again, assumed in calls for more green space, so orthodox that it's heretical to argue against it. But honestly, each piece of that equation is totally absurd. Even though the idea of "nature" has been comprehensively dismantled by scholars, "nature" discourses are central to maintaining the colonial apparatus of parks.

It doesn't require too much of a diversion into philosophies of the other-than-human world to suggest that there isn't all that much "natural" about parks, urban or otherwise. The road surrounding Bocce Ball Park is just as "natural" as the park: both are assemblages of non-human material, harvested, combined, recombined and moulded for specific and ideological human uses and pleasure. Bocce Ball Park requires just as much, maybe more, human intervention to survive; without huge amounts of work — vigilant supervision, construction and maintenance — the park — like all parks — would disappear.

The romantic view of nature and parks relies on a jumbled mess of ideas, most often developing a portrait of "nature" that is highly gendered, weak and pure, needing masculine protection to be "saved" by "eco-knights ready to save the helpless 'lady nature' from the dragon of human responsibility" (Heller 1999: 13). Alternatively, and often simultaneously, "nature" is described as terrifying, capricious and unpredictably dangerous, and humans require expansive protection from the depredations of the wild.

Few people who have been lost in the bush, caught in a storm at sea, suffered in the throes of a malarial fever, confronted with a powerful animal or subject to drought are prone to think of the other-than-human world as pathetic and helpless. But equally, few of us are keen to talk about "nature" as dangerously malignant: that hardly reflects the joys, meanings and deep satisfactions we realize from other-than-human encounters. Any attempts to deny the incomprehensible complexity and subjectivities of the other-than-human world become fodder for grim kinds of politics.

It is far better to talk about human/other-than-human intersections in *relational* terms. Adam Arola describes how easily people — from environmentalists, to hikers, to loggers, to nature enthusiasts — see the other-than-human world exclusively in terms of instrumentalized human desires, "framing its existence in terms of human purposes" (2011: 4). This objectification of the non-human is critical for social relations based on domination. The antidote is to think in terms of what Michi Saagiig Nishnaabeg scholar Leanne Betasamosake Simpson (2013) calls "respectful relations with plant and animal nations." It is unfamiliar to me to speak about plants and animals as "nations," but it strikes me as precisely the kind of insight that gives weight to relational claims. Thinking about parks, and especially Bocce Ball Park, through relational politics gives us some insight on what an ethical future might look like.

One route I have found occasionally useful is to think in terms of an entwined and historicized understanding of human/other-than-human connections. Then we can begin to speak not of authenticity, or of "nature" "improving" us (or vice versa), but of social and political choices. If the domination of the natural world by humans is predicated on the domination of humans by humans, then by subjectifying the non-human (say, by speaking of "plant and animal nations") in all its creative striving toward self-determination, we can ask what does an ethical, non-dominatory relationship with the other-than-human world look like? What do mutual and respectful relationships look like between humans and between humans and the other-than-human world? Parks in general, and certainly Bocce Ball Park, is as good a place as any to start experimenting.

Every definition of "nature" is really an argument for how people should be spending their time, how they should be interacting with the other-than-human, what activities are valuable and which should be extinguished. Our buddy tells an interesting story about coming back from hunting. He and his partner were pulled over by a wildlife conservation officer who carefully inspected what they were dragging home and concluded that, because they had not kept the horns and genitalia of the deer they had killed, they were afoul of the law, and the officer confiscated everything. Our friend wasn't that upset even though it was a significant volume of meat they had spent several days in the bush hunting. He agreed that they had not followed regulations carefully enough and that the consequences were legitimate. His only complaint that was no extractive industry in British Columbia is ever expected to adhere to anything like the kinds of standards that individual hunters are. If the logging, fishing, mining, oil and gas industries were subject to that level of regulation, supervision and monitoring, we'd be living in a far less polluted place. It is clear what kinds of human/other-than-human intersections get privileged, and they revolve mainly around capital.

The history of urban parks is one of landscaping and scenery, of utility and improvement, regulation and discipline. Parks claim to uplift people, that they are the best of the city, that they are the city-but-not-the-city, that they are essential for personal and social re-creation. There is so much to love about parks, but they need to be understood not as natural or authentic, but as restricted, ordered spaces that clearly articulate what constitutes correct behaviour and acceptable interactions. And that exercise is intensely political and biopolitical.

Parks are always performing certain sets of relations and thus are enmeshed within ongoing narratives of control and management, and Bocce Ball Park is hardly exempt. There are constellations of actors here all trying to assert themselves and order conduct. Homeowners trying to eject homeless people. Drinkers worrying that comrades are too rowdy. The woman telling me to "go home." Parents bossing their kids around, and kids refusing to listen. Bad Vlad. People camping. Bocce players occupying their runs. Dog owners refusing to leash their animals. Dudes yelling at passing women. Bureaucrats declaring which plants and animals have a right to stay. All of us are jostling for room and making claims, deploying a multitude of performative strategies to carve out space for certain kinds of relations. And it is one of the great pleasures of Bocce Ball Park that so many of those relations are naked and unapologetic.

When relations are in plain view, we can see and assess them: we can resist the dominatory or exploitative ones and nurture relationships based on respect and mutuality. But that everyday project is fundamentally corrupted when all our relationships rest on unadorned material histories of colonialism. Until very recently, Bocce Ball Park was exclusively Indigenous land, and it is now colonial space, claimed by the vagaries of professionalized state actors and sovereignties. But this presents us with some clear possibilities. If parks are supposed to "improve" us all, and if we are to have legitimate conversations about what that means, then surely, confronting Bocce Ball Park's colonial foundation is the correct starting point. If parks are the landed expressions of political rationalities, the grounds where "right conduct" is performed, we humbly suggest that decolonizing Bocce Ball Park is a fine place to begin. Parks can be common places, but only if that commonality acknowledges its history.

Maybe more than most places, and specifically because of their claims to commonality, parks can and should be subject to decolonizing efforts. Following Eve Tuck and C. Wayne Yang, I concur that any decolonization has to be about land (and all the power that land sovereignty implies): "Decolonization in the settler colonial context must involve the repatriation of land simultaneous to the recognition of how land and relations to land have always already been differently understood and enacted; that is, *all* of the land, and not just symbolically" (2012: 21). That is to say, I believe that the woman who confronted me in the park was correct in her critique. And facing up to that conversation, more than anything else I can think of, will improve us all.

Parks have long been a subject of deep resentment and frustration to many Indigenous people across the planet. All parks, and maybe especially large national parks, extol and encourage certain kinds of behaviour (sightseeing, hiking, tent camping, canoeing) while severely restricting and punishing other kinds (hunting, fishing, trapping, fish camps). These distinctions are not random; they are colonial ordering mechanisms, annexing Indigenous territory, and then despite claims to commonality and to "benefitting all people," denying Indigenous people access to their traditional practices. In that, parks are deployed as one more tool for genocide, and Bocce Ball Park, despite its modest size and ambition, contributes to that work. But it doesn't have to.

There have been some attempts to rethink park governance in Canada. For several decades now, various levels of park administrators have heard Indigenous critiques, and in some parks, especially in the North, attempts have been made at restructuring administration. There are many flavours and levels of these initiatives, typically named "co-management," but all of them attempt to bring Indigenous representatives into park resource management, land use and administrative decisions.[2] It might be argued that these invitations to participate in park governance are respectful and full of promise for Indigenous communities. And in some instances and sometimes, real successes have been achieved. For the most part though, co-management has become one more strategy for containing, prescribing, regulating and managing Indigenous lives. The grounds for discussion about parks are always based on highly limited possibilities, with the dominance of the Canadian state never in real question and power organized to maintain order. Indigenous people have been "invited to participate" in discussions about park management, but only in highly constrained debates — an invitation that ends up being worse than not being invited at all. Co-management is a dirty word for many, one more rhetorical trick that falls in the same basket as reconciliation, appeasement, assimilation, placation and consultation. Marc Stevenson (2004) argues: "It would be difficult to conceive of a more insidious form of cultural assimilation than co-management as currently practiced in northern Canada."

The deployment of parks as a mechanism of domination is hardly restricted to Canada. Across the globe, there are parks and conservation, preservation and protected areas that are mobilized to suppress Indigenous sovereignties. Consider the statement from Indigenous delegates at the Fifth World Parks Congress, held in South Africa in September 2003:

> The declaration of protected areas on indigenous territories without our consent and engagement has resulted in our dispossession

and resettlement, the violation of our rights, the displacement of our peoples, the loss of our sacred sites and the slow but continuous loss of our cultures, as well as impoverishment. It is thus difficult to talk about benefits for Indigenous peoples when protected areas are being declared on our territories unilaterally. First we were dispossessed in the name of kings and emperors, later in the name of State development and now in the name of conservation. (quoted in McKay and Caruso 2004)

This statement, among many others, lays bare the impossibility for any land to claim innocence. Territory is an expression of power. It may well be that it is fundamentally impossible for states to relinquish their white-knuckled grips on sovereign territorial claims. And certainly not without significant counter-force being exerted. But the failures of co-management and the dishonesty of conservation areas might contain within them an opening. There is a chance to learn from the failures of co-management practices in Canada and listen to Indigenous voices, and there is some evidence that maybe, just maybe, parks administrators in Vancouver are interested in those conversations.

Perhaps the best lesson to be gleaned from Canadian park practice is that the notion of a park is fundamentally unstable. Parks are relatively recent inventions, and we don't have to be trapped into a calcified and colonial rendition of what they might be. There are some honourable possibilities buried within all the dominant intentions and these ideas of parks are well worth hanging on to. It may be hard to hear that parks are not benign repositories of virtue and good conduct, and that they are reviled by so many, but we can remake this. The fact that parks claim to be common ground, despite all the contradictions within those claims, opens up a myriad of potentialities.

We can rethink and remake Bocce Ball Park, just like every other park. Here's one starting point for conversation: Why should Bocce Ball Park not be offered to the Musqueam (xʷməθkʷəy̓əm), Squamish (Sḵwx̱wú7mesh) and Tsleil-Waututh (səlilw̓ətaʔɬ) Nations? I know that's a facile construction of the question, but it's just to get us started. If we are really interested in decolonization, taking it seriously and not metaphorically, then we have to talk about land and territory. The park could be returned in a graduated, incremental manner with administration handed over to the three nations, if they are amenable. Perhaps the existing Parks Board apparatus could still be deployed, but in a different kind of collaborative arrangement, one that is grounded in respectful restitution. Maybe a council of elders could be convened as the sovereign authority in park decision-making, with the existing infrastructures under their purview. Why not? And while we're at it, why not return all city parks in the Vancouver Parks Board (VPB) system? There is some conversation underway in the VPB about co-management structures, but those discussions have to be pushed strongly in a legitimately decolonial direction.

This would surely take time, and all kinds of complications would arise, but it's just one city block. It has changed hands repeatedly over the past hundred-plus years; one more shift is hardly that big a deal. Leanne Simpson (2013) argues: "You know what, when an individual even within Canadian law steals a really expensive car and gets caught — they still have to give it back! They don't get to keep it even if it's worth a lot of money and they really like it." The City of Vancouver illegally acquired stolen property when they assumed control of Bocce Ball Park. But we can rectify that. Decolonization is the irreplaceable and inescapable first step for talking about commonality. If parks are supposed to improve us, surely that's the only place to start.

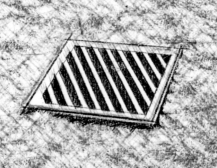

3

SAME TIME,
SAME PLACE

Bocce Ball Park
in 2015

CONTESTED, CLAIMED, CHRONICLED
– A YEAR WITH BOCCE BALL PARK

This is a photo essay drawn from a set of 365 images that I, Daisy, took of the park between January 1 and December 31, 2015. I hope that these 22 photos illustrate what becomes clear as you flick through all 365 images — how it is both a place in itself (messy and beautiful, populated and deserted, in flux and maintained into a state of semi-sameness) and a place that facilitates the many activities and lives of the people who spend time here and pass through it.

These photos were taken largely on my walk to school during the end of my grade 12 year, but there are also many that were taken at night after I had almost forgotten to take a picture that day, some on early summer mornings before work and others at times when something interesting was happening in the park such as a celebration or an eclipse. Matt, Selena and Sadie, as well as many wonderful friends, roommates and neighbours, have all also taken some of these images as I went to university in the fall and my time near the park decreased and I thank them all greatly for helping me complete this project.

I think it is important that you see the place we are talking about in this book and see it together rather than simply scattered throughout these essays. Drawn together, these images show you the park throughout the year of 2015 and, I hope, ground the many stories and arguments that are outlined in this book.

* The full set of 365 colour images is available online on the Fernwood website (https://fernwoodpublishing.ca/resources/on-this-patch-of-grass).

47

Days 7 (top) & 46 (bottom)

Days 72 (top) & 108 (bottom)

Days 117 (top) & 123 (bottom)

Days 144 (top) & 168 (bottom)

Days 175 (top) & 180 (bottom)

Days 181 (top) & 186 (bottom)

Days 193 (top) & 195 (bottom)

Days 215 (top) & 240 (bottom)

Days 271 (top) & 274 (bottom)

Days 316 (top) & 317 (bottom)

Days 333 (top) & 365 (bottom)

4

THE PARK
GOERS

To me, Victoria Park is summer nights, after dinner, before bed, getting in one last go at the monkey bars. It is tired trudging through
rain at 8 a.m. with a heavy backpack on, heading to school. It is learning
to ride my bike. It is taking an illicit sip of booze knowing my parents
are sleeping uncomfortably close. It is running late. It is playing with a
babysitter as my sister hurtled her way into this world. It is sitting on
a bench, waiting to meet somebody. It is crying on the phone. It is a
perfect spiral on a football. It is a big dog running at me full tilt and
then swerving at the last minute. It is bumping into people I'd rather
not see. It is music drifting through my bedroom window. It is sirens;
it is "someone got knifed in the park." It is the whole neighbourhood
looking at the super moon, oohing and ahhing. It is muddy grass, a few
benches, gross washrooms, a pretty nice playground, a city block, a square
of land that has been there through the years, for me and my family, as
well as for countless others.

On any non-rainy day, Victoria Park is filled with all kinds of these
others doing all kinds of things. People playing music, reading, chatting,
kids on the playground, a bocce game, people drinking, playing cards,
dogs, any number of predictable and/or unpredictable activities. By any
account, it is a park that is used and loved by many people. And this
chapter is about listening to some of them. I set out to talk to people who
use the park. I wanted to find out what the park means and has meant
to them, how they've used it and what role it plays in their lives. I tried
to talk to people who are at least slightly representative of who uses the
park. In that goal I have failed in all kinds of ways. Many people I asked
were not willing to talk or did not have the time. Many people were

justifiably suspicious of me and the project: they politely declined, and neither you nor I will get to hear their perspectives on this place. I mourn these gaps, these silences, these mis/representations. Please think of these lacunae when reading the profiles. So many different people use the park on a daily basis, and I tried to get the perspectives of a wide spectrum of park goers, but of course these profiles are selective and limited.

People who agreed to talk were often people I had a connection with from the past, people my family has built relationships with over years of living near, and being in the park. I asked each person the same simple, fairly open-ended questions, and they often led us to surprising places. Each person has re-read their contribution and approved of it being included in the book.

Talking to people about the park was a charming, frustrating, interesting project. They were both more and less hesitant to talk than I expected. People were generous and suspicious, open and closed, we chatted in the cold on a bench, in their homes or in mine. I am so grateful for each and every person I spoke with for sharing their thoughts, experiences and time with me. I thank them for taking my questions about the park seriously, and for opening up about their lives.

Each person I spoke with has their own timeline of the park, of high and low points, of shifts and constants. Each person has their own view of when the park is at its best and worst, their own narrative of change — their own version of the most ideal park and of the least ideal. Not surprisingly, there were many different perspectives and to me, there was more divergence than cohesion. Some park goers adamantly assured me that the neighbourhood used to be more family friendly, and some told me that it used to be rife with conflict, drug-use and crime, and only now is becoming more calm. Some saw the park as a peaceful space of tolerance where people from all different backgrounds coexist, and others described to me a place in which people rub up against one another often in less than pleasant ways. And I of course have my own views and experiences of the park, and sometimes squaring them up with conflicting views from others was difficult. There really is no narrative to present, or consensus to be had. I offer these profiles as intersecting strings of experience coming from and going to many different places. These strings cross each other at various times and places, usually in the park. In many

Victoria Park, day 68. Photo by Daisy Couture

ways, the park is an example of an inclusive, diverse and useful public space in which people live out their lives together despite difference. In other ways, it is a place of inequity, tension and power struggles.

The park is located about a block from a government-run liquor store on the main drag, Commercial Drive, and, perhaps consequently, or perhaps coincidentally, there are often groups of people hanging out and drinking in one corner of the park. These are racialized groups, often Indigenous or Latinx people, sometimes homeless or seemingly so, and they are a fixture in the park, hanging out, playing games and drinking. Despite not asking anyone about drinking in the park, nearly everyone I talked to mentioned it. Obviously drinking — who does it, when, where, how and why — is an issue that is close to the surface for people who use and live near to Victoria Park. Many of the people I interviewed felt uncomfortable with the drinking in the park, for a variety of reasons, many of which are understandable. However, in addition to these concerns, I found that issues about drinking in the park tended to be code for race and class-based assumptions about who and what the park is meant for. Almost everyone who took issue with alcohol use in the park *also* admitted to drinking in the park themselves. Many of the park goers had no problem with middle-class people having a beer after work in the sun, but they did have a problem with groups of people drinking in the day. The time, place, type, and results of drinking loom large in the dynamics of the park, with each park goer having a unique and complex web of boundaries and standards of acceptability. Some thought drinking was fine as long as it was in the evening; for others it's fine as long as the bottle is in a paper bag. Some thought it was fine as long as you don't get drunk; others said that it's fine over by Victoria Drive, but not close to the playground. The goers articulated to me individualized boundaries of respectability, informed by their backgrounds and social positions. What was often left unsaid was historical and contemporary regimes which have shaped these boundaries and the places of different bodies in relationship to them. The park goers aren't ignorant though. They know about inequality, and for the most part they care about it, but day-to-day, they have their limits, and drinking is a place where it seems these limits are consistently in conflict. And drinking in parks is not illegal everywhere. In other places I've lived (Montreal, Copenhagen), it's perfectly legal and socially acceptable to drink in public parks. Social tensions coalesce elsewhere of course, but in Victoria Park, it's *all* about who drinks what, where and when. At stake in the park are the boundaries of respectable drinking, and almost everyone I spoke to spontaneously mentioned it.

Closely tied to issues of drinking were dynamics of entitlement which emerged throughout the project. Most people I spoke to communicated to me a sense of entitlement to the park, a feeling that the park was somehow *theirs* to use, to share, to police, and to enjoy. The park goers I talked to have come to this park from many different places: Winnipeg, Burma, Italy, Saskatchewan, El Salvador, other parts of Vancouver. Most park goers I spoke to are visitors: they and their families come to the park with so many different experiences, being pushed and pulled around the globe. Other park goers are not settlers. They and their families have been here for millennia and this place isn't unique in that Indigenous people use and care for this park regularly. However they've come to this patch of grass, everyone I spoke with has made a life in and around the park. They use it and care for and about it, and each person has their own ideas about what and who the park is meant for. Historical shifts in entitlement to this land are not in the forefront of the minds of the park goers, although ideas about public space, common goods and collective ownership are. The park goers have made this place theirs in many different ways, and this entitlement has two sides to it; the care, the ownership, the joy people feel for the park, as well as the exclusion, the righteousness and the friction I have seen between users.

While the park is a beautiful example of a symbiotic sharing of space in the face of difference, the park is also a venue for the enactment of our world's most pernicious regimes of power. Colonialism, patriarchy and white supremacy are alive and well in Victoria Park. Women get yelled at, cops selectively question, fine and bully, racial slurs are hurled, violence is semi-regular, and almost nobody talked to me about the park being Indigenous land. The park has been for some, a place of fear, of frustration, of anger, as well as a venue to carve out space for themselves and their communities in the face of these struggles. In this way I see Victoria Park as a place of resistance, of daily protest and of navigations of power. Most people I spoke with mentioned the park as a site of negotiation, a space occupied and used by lots of people in a balancing act of needs and wants. In some ways, the wild diversity of uses and occupations of this patch of grass may point toward a hopeful horizon of sharing land in a decolonial context. In general, people love this park and the part it plays in their lives. Victoria Park is simple and complex; it is a place of tension, of joy, of friction, of connection, of difference, of power, of protest. A frustrating place, but by most accounts a good place, a place worth being, a place worth knowing, a place worth caring about. But, of course, that is how I see it, and I invite you to read about how others see it.

Lucy

Lucy grew up off the park in the 1970s and 1980s. For many years she lived near the park with her two older children, with their father, and later her partner. She now has younger children and no longer lives in the area, but her mother, sister and other family members continue to live nearby. She has fond memories of being in the park throughout many different phases of her life.

"In terms of the area where the park is, I moved there when I was eight or nine. So I spent a lot of time there with my friends. And then, I still lived in that area when Alicia and Nolan [Lucy's older kids] were born. I spent a lot of time with them playing there. And now, I now bring my next set of kids, 20 years later. Also, I would bring my dogs there a lot. Rachel [Lucy's sister] and I both had dogs when we were little, and that's actually how I met the kids' dad. I feel like that park has just been a place where lots of memories [have happened]. I mean gosh I remember, I mean this is kind of embarrassing, but I remember being drunk and falling off the swing there as a teenager!"

Lucy has vivid memories of playing in the park as a kid. She balanced on the frames of the bocce ball courts, climbed on the monkey bars and did dance routines with her friends. "They had that structure that had an angled roof, and we used to climb on top of [it], and it was the most awesome thing because you could climb and sit on the top, so good for the slightly older kids so they could sit and smoke or whatever. I really enjoyed sitting on that roof. I wish that was still around. That was a fun thing to climb. And maybe partly 'cause it wasn't meant to be climbed. You felt kind of strong and like you could get up to the top and sit on the roof and it felt kinda cool. I feel like there's a lot of independence in that park for me so those are really good memories. I never felt scared in that park. When I was growing up there I never remember feeling any fear."

Lucy views the park as continuing to be a place where many different people gather, but she sees the interactions among users as mainly good. "I had one run-in with a bocce ball person that got mad because my dog ran over and smelled him, and I remember I didn't react very well. I was kind of cocky with him. But for the most part I got along with everybody in the park. It was used for so many things. It's always had a lot of different groups, sub groups; there's people who are just sitting and hanging out, and there's people playing in the park with their kids, and there's people playing bocce ball and everybody does their own thing.

"I guess, there's also been some fear in that park, like my brother, who is younger than me, saw a man get his head smashed in with a bat in that park. And, there's a lot of drug use and alcohol use. I would say more alcohol, in that park. I mean I've been one to use alcohol in that park! I remember when there was a lot of really loud, drunk, kind of aggressive energy coming from that park. I feel like it has changed, and I think they've had more police presence. So, for good or for bad, that's what I've noticed."

Now, Lucy interacts with the park mainly as a parent to young children. "I do really like the new [playground area] that they've built for kids. It's really, really a nice space, and it feels very contained, but really big still, so there's lots of room to run around but it gives me sort of a sense of, kind of, I can see where everybody is. I like that they've moved it away from the busier road. I feel like they've put a little more care into Victoria park in the way that they designed it. They've got a lot of more spaces. It's unfortunate, if I lived in the neighbourhood, we'd probably use it daily. But because we live so much further away, we hardly use it now."

The park has been somewhat of a constant for Lucy throughout her life. "I don't have a specific word or feeling; it's a familiar place. It's a place that a lot has happened. I mean, honestly, I can go back to sitting in it with my friends, playing hooky from school, to right now, and I am the grown-up with my kids, giving them snacks and watching them on the slide. And then also in the middle, passing out on a swing, drunk. I've grown up in that park. And then the two sets of kids. So I have mixed feelings about some of what's happened there, but mostly just lots of good memories. I've always loved that park. That park has always been close to where I've ended up at different times. It's just been there."

Rusty

Rusty was born in Winnipeg and moved to Vancouver twenty-five years ago. He has found community in East Vancouver and mainly uses the park as a social space.

"It's been a real growth process, definitely. Vancouver has taught me a lot about Canada. 'Cause going from Winnipeg and seeing certain possibilities, and going to Vancouver and seeing other possibilities, and all the while there being struggle, and not in any way light struggle. It's quite a strange experience."

Rusty used to go to Grandview Park mainly, but since the renovations, he has shifted to Victoria Park, which he calls the "Other Park" — it's not Grandview. "Smoking weed and drinking [is what he does in the park].

But mostly because that's the social place to do it. It used to be that you could just exist in Grandview Park, and actually, there was some time that was so paradise-like. I just remember the whole park would be full of all these people sprawled out in the sun, drinking and smoking and being so pleasant. They ruined it. So then all of a sudden, I am more into this park."

Rusty really values the park as a green space in the city and worries that it might be developed. He's even heard rumours about it. "It's so strange how there's not really a lot of [green space in] Vancouver. They are gradually whittling down the green space. It's what is happening. That place is getting more and more important. If some stupid contractor decides to make eyes at it, the next thing you know it's going to be half the size. I actually think I did hear some story about contractors that were surveying it or whatever, who laughed at the suggestion that they weren't going to able to turn it into condos. I mean I don't know how I heard that story. Hopefully they don't ruin everything here. That's what I mean, over all that time, you do see how much it changes. It just keeps going and going, and yeah, there's a lot of weird little agendas."

Rusty didn't have a space like the park in Winnipeg. He thinks the cops would have bothered him. "You always kind of find a little place, or a little spot under a rock or something like that, but realistically no, Winnipeg is like, no. I mentioned that it [the park] was about drinking and smoking, those things aren't legal in Winnipeg. I mean they're not 100 percent legal here either, but the cops [would have bothered him] when I was growing up! By now, it's like kind of, the same thing, everybody's pretty hip to, you know, police brutality" But generally, Rusty says he doesn't have many problems with the cops. "Not in the park no. I don't like them, but I don't even attract them, or seem like I would do stuff that needed their attention."

Overall, the park is a place where Rusty feels the community and has conversations that he cares about. "I like the community there. Instead of the kind of conversations that are very erasable, you can have a conversation [and] keep that for the next ten years or whatever, and look back on it. One of the things that really struck me from what my friend [talked about in a video Rusty made], society basically just condones bullying women. And that's society. It's the same thing. I find that being Black has been so crazy because there's all this stuff that's put on you, and there's all this stuff that you can volunteer for, but, I know it just is not very helpful ultimately. It is weird like that with women, because women have this thing of people are telling them what they're like."

Rusty appreciates the people in the park a lot. He sees people going through hard things but still bravely speaking their minds. "The degree of courageous speakers; some people just can't handle the truth, that's the bottom line. I am trying to figure out how to make sure that it turns. The people, that there's a door that opens somehow. But I don't know that alcohol is going to do anything for anybody for a long time, so, I don't have a lot of hope in that regard. There's people all just in fool's gold world and they just can't help themselves. We do have to change if we want to keep our people."

Overall, Rusty thinks people in the park get along well. "It's a really neat park for that. Everyone's so cordial. They have all the toys. Any crooked parent should just go there at night, scoop all the toys, Christmas Eve, like load under your tree for Christmas morning 'cause I am telling you, that is like, Toys R Us over there. And nobody does anything. I even saw a little dart gun! It was like, this is definitely in the stealable category; this is not like a choo-choo or a Fisher Price dump truck. This is actually cool for adults too!"

"[The park is] a really magical place. It is. And it reflects the magic of this strange community. So it's not random magic; it's very specific and special and unpredictable."

Winston

Winston Jang has lived off the park for fifty-one years. He grew up here with his parents and grandparents, and continues to live in his family home, now with his wife, children and mother. He has fond memories of the neighbourhood from his youth, but noticed a dramatic change in the park when the liquor store opened just one block away. Now his relationship with the park is more tense, and he has been thinking about moving in recent years. He says "I've seen a lot of changes in the park."

Winston has good memories of growing up in the neighbourhood, when Italian families were the demographic majority. "The neighbourhood was completely family-orientated. Everybody knew one another. I recall neighbours being so friendly and inviting. I had friends in the neighbourhood where grandmas, mums would always call us in to eat lunch, dinner, whatever, and we did the same thing to them. So really, [I'm] Asian-born, but grew up like an Italian in many ways. The European culture is very similar to our culture."

Winston remembers a huge shift in the neighbourhood when the liquor store opened. "Oh we really used the park. And we were creative — didn't have obviously what the park has to offer now — we would swing on the trees, just like carefree kids, just play! Hide-n-seek, tag, we played football, baseball, we did everything! I probably remember doing that until about the age of ten. When all of a sudden the whole neighbourhood sort of shifted. The community was never given an option as to whether we were going to allow the so-called dreaded liquor store to come in. It just popped up one day. No longer did we play in the park the way we used to. No longer did people leave their doors wide open, unlocked. Chances are, growing up, we probably would have used it less anyways, but still it was almost an immediate thing."

Winston continues to feel the loss of the park. "It got to the point where we felt like outsiders really, because the park was no longer ours. We grew up a little quicker, seeing all this happening around us. I feel ripped off. Having to go somewhere else to play, when that park should have been rightfully ours to play in. I've lost my so-called entitlement to the park. I also feel bad cause my kids never got to use the park growing up."

The park is source of conflict in Winston's life. "I call the police every day. So that's frustrating, and I feel that the local police force has not done a good enough job in preserving the park. There are a lot of young families moving back into the neighbourhood. What do you see nearby? These guys, right? My kids lost out on it but I am pretty determined. I am going to make it difficult for these guys. It's the bane of my existence. These guys. I feel sorry for all the young'uns that have grown up in the area because you didn't get to really appreciate the area as much as potentially you could have, or should have."

Despite living in the same place his whole life, the tensions in the neighbourhood have made him consider moving. "[There's] really a sadness that has crept in for living in the neighbourhood. I will always consider it to be home, 'cause there is so much that living off the Drive has to offer. It's an amazing place to live! Really, the only reason why we stay now is because of mum. She knows the merchants down the Drive. She does her walks every day down the Drive. She walks the neighbourhood; she looks forward to it. But she hates looking out the front window, sitting on the porch. See, if my mum wasn't alive, we would be gone."

"Do I love the neighbourhood? Yes. Do I hate the neighbourhood? Yes. I am torn. My boys do not want to move. 'Cause to them it's still home. But they also hate what's happening in front of the house. When no one's in the park, Kyle, Brandon, and myself will go out, we will throw the ball around. But we typically think of going elsewhere. We will go there in a pinch. I will take my nephews to the park to play, take advantage of the playground because they are that age, but really, I probably spend less than 5 percent of my time in the park now, as opposed to like almost 100 percent [when he was a kid]. I call it the pit. It's a term of endearment a bit, but I also think it's the pit too because after the Parks Board re-did the park, the turf is worse now than it ever was, for drainage."

Nevertheless, Winston has fond memories of and in the park. "I remember teaching my best friend, who was my neighbour, how to ride a bike. I had him in the middle of the park. I forgot to teach him how to stop — 'cause back then it's an old mustang, no hand brakes, just foot brakes. I never taught him how to stop so the dummy rolled straight into the bushes! We were dying laughing; he went full bore right into the bushes! Little memories like that, it still brings a laugh, a smile to my face, 'cause that's the innocence that we had. That's what the park gave us."

"Whether we ever get down to moving or not, it'll always have a really, really fond place in my heart. Because I will always think of myself as an East End kid who grew up by Victoria Park! My older brothers and sisters still feel the same way."

Luigi's parents ran a grocery store across the street from the park. He spent a lot of time there as a kid

Luigi

"I grew up in that park. The Italian bocce players frequented the park as well, buying their cigarettes, pops, mainly sending the kids like me, or the other neighbourhood kids to go run errands and getting a two cent or a five cent tip. We lived daylight hours in that grocery store. Although we lived up the street, we had our meals there, and we took turns as customers came in, we were trying to eat in the back and we just basically went around the table who went out. And as a child I had limits to what I would do so I would end up calling my mom or dad anyway, or my reluctant baby sister! To come take over, slicing some meats or whatever was required."

"You couldn't play hockey in the park, so we played on the street. A block away, either right on Semlin or Salsbury. But we played baseball in there, football, soccer. Depending on the season. And hide-n-seek sometimes in the evenings, on Saturdays in the summertime. On the far end, on the Salsbury side there was a, kind of, a walled-off area that had been a lawn-bowling club. And then it got abandoned and we would break through the fence and get inside and the lawn got mowed so it was a good area to play soccer — or baseball. 'Cause if you hit it over the fence you got a home run! If you hit it into the bush it was a two-base hit! I remember having firecrackers, and then the cops chasing one of my friends, and he went against the back hedge, the dark hedge, and he turned his coat inside out because he had a dark coat on — a dark lining, and he just sort of pinned himself against the hedge and he never got caught; he got away!"

"I like the fact there's people in it [the park]. And I think by putting the playground in there, you've got families in there, you've got people who frequent it. It's always had that element of colour — the liquor store being fairly close. You pick up, go buy the booze, and go hang out by the park. I've never had, or know any incidents with the people drinking there. The people who tend to drink there usually tend to just drink and hang out. There's never been any fighting or anything like that or they certainly don't bother anyone else with kids. I lived in the area while I had young kids as well, and I think at that point there was a swing set and little else!"

"Probably the 1960s and then all through the 70s. Probably in the 90s it faded. Because the younger kids didn't play, and the older ones just got too old. All I know is it was very funny when they put them [bocce courts] in because nobody used them. 'Cause nobody actually asked the people who play bocce if they wanted bocce courts. I don't think they were ever used. I don't know if it's because they don't like the straightness of it or they like the idea of the challenge of the rough terrain. When you gotta be able to get around the mounds of the different dips and hills and — there's skill involved."

I spoke with Lillipilli and her mother Faith while playing in the park. Lillipilli was eight at the time, and they live close by. When I asked Lillipilli what she thought of the park she exclaimed, "FUN!"

Lillipilli

Faith: "And can you tell a little bit of the story, Lilpil, about this park. What's your name for this park?"

Lillipilli: "My park."

Faith: "Or didn't you call it Lillipilli park?"

Lillipilli: "I played there a lot. It was my favourite park. I play soccer with a ball, I run around. Oh yeah the first time I rode my bike it was around this park!"

Sadie: "Do you have any special memories in this park?"

Lillipilli: "Swinging on the swing. And getting very dizzy that I got so sick!"

Faith: "She got so sick she had dizzy-sickness for days."

Recently, Faith and Lillipilli heard there was a new piece of equipment at the park, and they were excited to use it. It's a red bucket that spins.

Lillipilli: "It's something that you sit in and it spins you round and round. It's fun! Because it makes you dizzy!"

Sadie: "Is there anything you don't like about the park?"

Lillipilli: "Too small!"

Sadie: "What do you wish it was?"

Lillipilli: "Waterpark!"

Sadie: "That would be really cool."

Faith: "Anything else?"

Lillipilli: "FUN! FUN! FUN! Fun fun fun fun fun fun fun."

Faith: "The main theme seems to be fun. But lots of first things happened here. Like first swings, first bike ride, first playing soccer happened here too with Papa. This park was kind of important."

Their family used to call the park "Lillipilli Park." "We used to come here all the time. We don't as much anymore, because she's at school, but prior to being in school, this was her park, right. Yeah, it's her park. It's not anyone else's park. It's her park. You know the way that kids are, right? They're just — the world revolves around them — it's called child-centred thinking."

Before she had a child, Faith didn't like parks. But, Lillipilli likes them and so their family spends a lot of time here. "I am not a park person, I'm not. I have recently become a park person because I have a child but prior to that I was never into parks. I used to really hate parks in fact, in my twenties. Because I was a radical. And so, parks were just, like landscaped spaces, and I just hated landscaped spaces. Even in cities I just thought things should be left wild. I like things that are derelict, I like things that are wild, possibly a little bit yucky for regular folks. So these kind of things just seem kind of manicured, safe spaces and I hated them. Now I have a child and it's different. [Parks were] eye-numbingly boring for me. But she loves it, so, that's what I did. Here we are. I remember it [Victoria Park] before the change as well. And I am not sure that the change is better. To be honest. I've been thrilled [with] the recent addition of gardens to parks. I love that. I love that they have started to do that 'cause that kind of bringing — I know that gardens are agricultural spaces as well but there is something wild and untrammelled about them still."

Joe

Joe grew up off the park, and spent lots of time there as a kid, teen, and now as a young adult.

"I am Joe. Joe Abbott. I live in East Van. I am a musician, I play jazz, I like to travel, I hang out. I've been going to the park for as long as I can remember going anywhere. And the park when I was a kid was just the place to go. The corner store and the park were the first two places that we were allowed to go on our own, so, it was really fun. We would go and get Freezies for 50 cents."

Joe and his friends had lots of names for the park and each other. "When I was a kid we always called it Bocce Park, as well as Vic Park, Vicky C, it rhymes with Tricky Z, as well as of course Micky Spee [McSpadden Park] and ah yeah Micky Spee holds it down — it's not as good as Victoria Park — it's good, sure it is, it's great, but ya know, I like Victoria Park better."

When the park was under construction, Joe felt the loss. "What I do remember is that it seemed like a really long time. And I was really pissed off that they were doing it. And it just seemed like it was taking way too long. And I also thought that all the facilities were great, and like I didn't, you know, I didn't give a fuck. Like, why would they change the park, it was fine! It's a great park still. I always thought it was a little too suave, like, when they did it."

Joe had some formative experiences in the park and has met some important people in his life there. "When I became a teenager, we would come and hang out here and find people to buy us liquor. Anyway, it worked fine. And so I ended up meeting quite a few of the local park people. Like Niko. And Pablo! My swing guitar mentor. We basically met here in the park and he started showing us a bunch of stuff about how to play jazz guitar and so that was really cool. It's really mellowed out for me and my relationship to the park. Kinda learn how to do it a little better. It really was a little wild, me and the park."

Joe feels strongly that himself, his friends and all others should be able to use the park in the ways they see fit. "A park is a designated loitering space. Like, it is the only space that you are legally allowed to loiter 'cause you're not loitering if you are in a park, you're just doing the park thing." Joe doesn't like the tension between some homeowners in the area and the people he affectionately calls the "home bums" (people, some homeless, some not, who gather in the park to socialize, play games, and use drugs and alcohol). "It's funny, did ya see that there was an article in the paper complaining about the home bums? Basically, this article was just I guess some of these, like, 'Friends of Grandview Park' assholes had, like, made a complaint, well, probably several complaints about how there was people drinking in the park. It's just really goofy. I don't know, like, these guys have really never bothered me or anyone else I know, and also, if you look at the other people in the park, there's lots of people who drink at the park. It's really not a bad thing, drinking in the park! It's all in the same field [category of] leisure activities! Hang out with your friends, playing croquet, drinking a beer — it's really not all that bad! Once in a while there will be a very drunk person, but those people are that these, like, also usually mentally ill and just marginalized and fucked out of the system. I guess that's what I don't like about the park. That on rare occasions, there will be someone who is tripping out who is not on my level. People who are sick that no one cares to help. But that's really not even worth considering as a problem for myself because it's really not a problem for me. It's a problem for other people."

Joe dislikes the police presence in the park, and the selective policing that he sees. "Sometimes the cops come here. I really don't like that. That's a really bad part of the park! It's not the park's fault, but the cops! Sometimes they'll come by on a Friday evening or something like that, and there will be people, like young people that have nice things and are just good kids or whatever, that are drinking in the park, and they'll look over them, and they'll fuck with those guys. And that bugs me! That's what the police do, they get to choose who they fuck with and they fuck with the home bums. These guys rep the park harder than anyone else does. This is really what gives this park character. People think they are loitering, people try to say that they are loitering, but they are just [here] more often than anyone else! You can't loiter in a fucking park! They are playing cards and playing bocce and smoking weed. I like the people who use the park. I always feel comfortable here."

Jocelyn lives with her husband Ian, and their three children in North Vancouver, quite far from the park. However, they used to live nearby.

Jocelyn

"One of the reasons we moved from Commercial Drive is that we needed a bit more space and we just couldn't get space there for the amount of money we had to spend. Another reason was the nature part of it. I wanted to able to walk to the forest and go to beaches without having to trek across the city, so that's why we moved. But we still go back to Commercial Drive, and my kids want to go to that [Victoria] park."

The park was a social space for Jocelyn and her young family. "It was our place where we met tons of families. Just so many people! Friends that are for life now, I met at that park. Swings, sandbox, and I love how there's like a big kid area and a small kid area. My little kids were small at that time so they felt really safe there. I, like, sometimes in the evenings would say, "let's make a community dinner" so people would just bring a picnic and we would meet there because it's so central … and that happened really spontaneously. There are other parks nearby, like there's Trout Lake, and like I said Grandview, but they just didn't have the same feel. I don't know what it was. I think it was just because it was a smaller park, yet it was so big because it attracted so many people. I was there every day. I was probably there in the morning, and after naps, for like, the longest time. I met *so* many friends. I think I would still go to that park to just sit and read a book or something, because whenever I go, I still see people I know."

Sometimes Jocelyn felt uncomfortable in the park especially with some of the dogs. "So it was great. But then it started to change. It started to become an off-leash area for dogs. There was this group of guys who had some feral dogs. They were sleeping in the park. They were really nice guys, and they would always introduce themselves and always introduce their dogs, but these dogs would run wild in the park. So we put out our picnic blanket one day, and these dogs came running — as dogs do — and kind of gave my older child a scare for her life. So we didn't go on the green grass area any more after that. I was never scared of the dogs, and my husband said those feral dogs are probably better trained than some of the dogs on leash, because they know their limits, like they are not going to attack you, but if they see food, then they are going to try to go for it. And I was, like, "I am not happy with this, I don't care if they are feral or trained, don't matter, I am not going!" So for a while there we couldn't walk down the path, where these dogs were, we had to walk around the park."

Some of the people there also made her uncomfortable. "I hate to be negative, but some of the crowd that gathered at the left hand side is, you know, the usual, and then there was this drinking crowd that started to show up. Every now and then, the swearing and the physically drunk at 10 o'clock in the morning was a bit much to handle, and hard to explain to my daughter. There was this one time this guy was, like, wavering, and I wasn't sure which way he was going to fall, and I didn't want to scare my daughter either, but I was scared because I was pregnant.

"There was a period I felt unsafe. It was weird because it was like mid-week, and I think it was springtime, and I just had this feeling that it just wasn't right — like that much drinking to go on that early in the day — this party mentality almost, and nobody that I recognized, so I think it must have been people that were just passing through the city or got abandoned from another park, got kicked out. They clearly didn't know the dynamics of the park, like, you don't yell at your friend from across the way, and don't talk to me, like, they were saying names like 'Oh hi there hot mama! Where are you off to today?' So I was kind of avoiding that park, and then it peaked! There was an incident, and then all those people were gone! That problem, it was cleaned up. And I wouldn't say it was a problem, if they are just in their own space, but when they are starting to bother other people, and there were fights going on between groups of people. But we drank at the park too, it's not like we didn't go and take our beers. That was fine, but it was just when it was becoming a problem, that's when it felt unsafe."

Victoria Park has a particular swing that is important to Jocelyn and her family. "We call it Blue Swing Park 'cause I think it's the only park that has the black baby swing, and then there's a blue swing that has a back, so a baby and a toddler can go on at the same time, and it's the only park in the city that has that! Or in Greater Vancouver, 'cause there's not one in North Van! When I had a six-month-old and a two-and-a-half-year-old, it was like "oh my goodness!" So that's called Blue Swing Park, and that's why we keep going back, because my middle one loves Blue Swing Park!"

Now, living in North Vancouver, Jocelyn and her family go to their local park. "We go down the street, yeah Mohan Park. It's different. They don't play so much on the structure, but the space around it, so they want to roll down the hill, or collect acorns or pine cones. We often go into the forest and walk along that. The apparatus is interesting; it's made for really young kids, and then there's a park for older kids, so it's not really well designed, but having said that, she can go down and ride her bike all around."

At this point, Ian, Jocelyn's husband came home and joined in on the conversation. He finds Victoria Park to be quite different from Mahon Park. "I don't find I come across the same people. I mean I am not in the parks as often here, but I can't say that I've remembered recognizing someone more than once there."

Jocelyn: "Victoria Park was different, everyone says hello to you there. Everyone talks to you. I think it's also because you assume that everyone lives around you there. Whereas some of the parks here I don't think I get that. People drive to it or come 'cause of the trails. We used to go to the park a lot, but now they can just play in the backyard. Which in this phase of my life is easier 'cause I can do the dishes, and they can just play. I don't have to pack up and leave, pack up, pack up, pack up — I was getting tired of that. Even if we went across the street, I used to have to pack everything."

Ian: "There's a lot of the park that I don't miss but there's a lot that I do, because I don't have anything like that over here where at least I can know on a weekend I will take my kids there and have conversations with people I know that I would also consider friends."

Jocelyn: "It's the people. I was just telling her that. That's one thing I miss. All the people there."

Ian: "I loved the park and most days it was great, and I do miss it. I didn't really mind, you know I don't really mind the dogs and stuff, but when probably once a month there would be a fight, whether it's a fist-fight or swearing, and it's just not really something I wanted to explain to my kids.

I never wanted anybody to leave the park. I would never say that this park doesn't belong to these people, or these people, but I just thought that there, maybe at times, needed to be more respect for some of the different groups. Unfortunately, I think everybody is the same in that, have a few drinks and your awareness of respect, or your care for it, decreases. So, little things like drinking at the playground. If they had gone to the other side of the park, I wouldn't even have thought twice. If they had kind of taken it elsewhere or kept it over there it wouldn't be such a big deal. My theory on it, to make it [the park] good for everyone is just makes sure that nobody abandons it, you know, like keep everyone there, and keep everyone in check. I feel like it's a space that needs to be balanced. It's just finding the balance is a challenge."

Jocelyn: "There was a lot of fun impromptu things. I always remember coming and I'm sitting in my house and my mom comes and she's like, 'Don't take the girls to the park today' — and she's like an older, you know, conservative Indian woman, and I am like, 'Why?' and she is like, 'There's women — boobs everywhere!'"

Ian: "It was the Dyke March!"

Oscar is a painter, originally from El Salvador. He came to Canada in 1984 and at different points has lived near to the park. He comes to the park most days to socialize, play games, and drink.

Oscar

"I came to live on Kitchener from the English Bay Hotel. They gave us two weeks to find a place. Somebody said, "There is an area, there are Italians, and go and maybe you will like it." So that's why I came to live here, and since then, I like it. It's my barrio. So even if I leave, I always come back. Now I live close to Trout Lake, and I still feel I am in the barrio, in the borough."

"I like it because it's the place where we can gather. People, we speak the same language. Before we used to hang out at Grandview Park, but for totally different things. Now we do more physical or sporty stuff. We have a chance to get together and talk our language and do the things we do. We need that kind of communication. Between people from the same countries. I mean we are not from the same country but we are neighbours. We speak the same language, and that's the thing. I come to the park to have fun. Some people come from Surrey. I don't think everyone lives around here, just a few people. But because like I told you before, we need to be [with] our own."

A lot of Oscar's time in the park is spent playing bocce. "Now that they've fixed the new bocce ball [courts], now we are practising more or playing more, bocce ball, not football. Before, we were just spectators to the Italians playing, [but] we started playing maybe six years ago. We started playing on the old lanes, now we are playing daily. So that's become the new game for us. I come to the park, two to three times a week, and I am getting a little bit better [at bocce] because I like it. It reminds us of playing with marbles. Actually, [I've done] five or six paintings of glass marbles, and I like it because they are hard to paint, very hard to do the glass effects and the transparency, so I love it!"

Oscar sees a difference between people's activities in Victoria Park and some parks downtown. "It's different than here, it's different community, different people. I think people come here because the environment is kind of different. The same, sometimes bad behaviour, because people smoke cigarettes, people smoke dope, and some people drink beer, but we are not supposed to drink in the park."

Oscar doesn't like how some of his group litter and disrespect the park. He feels some tension about how his group acts. "Even if I drink, I don't like the way other people drink! I complain but, they don't listen. The thing I am doing, just picking up the bottles and empties, that's the thing I don't like about my own. My own people. Because sometimes we joke about [crows] because they are always together, right, but they kind of look like us, we are always together, and fight and shouting. It's our culture. We are a little bit loud.

"[I don't like] the way we behave. 'Cause some people, not all of them, some people do things that they don't supposed to do. Like peeing! But, I started to consider because they are older guys. We are missing some toilets or some portable thing. But that one is up to the City Hall. In general, I like what is going on. I mean the big children's site, we have our own lanes. I think I liked it before, I liked the design before [the renovations]. There were three lanes, and one was under the trees, with some benches. I think the guy who renovated it didn't know much about how to do it. But this is secondary stuff. I mean there is no drainage, that's another thing."

The park has undergone some redesigns. Tables were put in, and then taken out, and now there is just one big table with a purposefully non-functional roof structure on top. "Before, the way they designed it, there were lanes and there were tables. And we used to use the tables for playing cards and sometimes checkers. There were a lot of people coming. People who were homeless, those people who always looks brown and with dogs, those guys who live on the streets. They were different than us. I mean the way they behave, they were more loud and they got drunk and they look more dirty. So that's why City Hall took the tables. We don't have tables. But we do have the larger one." Oscar would really like to have a roof over the big table. "In summer it's hot, and when it's wet and we always talking about the City. Why they don't wanna put nothing on top? Because it means people will come to sleep or stay there illegally or something. So they don't want to."

For Oscar, the dynamics between groups are mainly relaxed. "There are Italian seniors and we are the Latinos. Before, only Italians played bocce. But after years and after they renovated, now we are more Latinos playing bocce and some Italians come play with us. So there's no fights, it's nothing like that. There are two lanes. If, sometimes there are four Italians who want to play, nobody say nothing. We let them to play. We are now the majority playing bocce and they are playing cards. So there's no fighting for space."

Oscar is bothered by the actions of some of "his own," but he doesn't know if there's anything he can do about it. "I think we are okay. The only thing is we need is to behave better. That's the thing. Some people. That is the thing. They give us a bad reputation. That's the only thing. That's it. I talk with other people and I say, 'I don't think the Hindu community is doing the same like us, you know, go to the Philippines, or I go to the White.' I see myself from other, 'We are the only one doing that, we are the one drinking on the park.' I go to different parks with my bicycle and I don't see anybody doing what we are doing, especially drinking. I drink myself, but I keep my wine in the bag. There was an article in the newspaper, the guy says 'Oh this is a park that always is Cinco de Mayo.' That was kind of a small article, but they put us in a situation that's 'Oh, we Latinos are doing that,' giving the whole park [a bad] name. That's the only thing, but there's no way to fix that, no telling them what to do."

This woman did not want to be identified by name. She felt uncomfortable with her comments being public but wanted to be honest in her interview. She has lived in the area with her daughter and husband for fifteen years. Her relationship with the park has mainly centred around her daughter, first playing there with her as a small child, and now worrying about her experiences there as a young woman.

"We've seen the park go through various phases and changes and stuff like that. When [my daughter] was younger we used the playground, and then as she got older she would just go with her friends and go by herself. As a teenager, she doesn't use the park, and I don't use the park. However, because we are right across from the park — we sit on our porch *a lot* so we see what's going on at the park. We don't really use the park, but we watch the park a lot."

She doesn't feel safe in the park and worries about her daughter's safety in the park. "We walk through the park, but I tell [my daughter] not to walk through the park at night. I don't feel like it's a safe park. It's a dealer park. We see deals happening all the time, and we get stuff hidden in the bushes, all the time. It doesn't really bother me all that much, but I see it happening. The thing that does bother me is that, now, there's a whole group of drunk guys that start drinking at pretty much noon. I feel unsafe walking by them. Like you know that those guys are looking you up and down. I think they could really deal with the park in a different way. I don't know how I would solve it. It seems like a lot was pushed from Grandview Park into this park when they re-did Grandview Park so they were just sort of moving problems around the neighbourhood."

However, there are some aspects of the park she appreciates. "On the other hand, in the summertime, it's really nice, 'cause you see people with their dogs, throwing a frisbee around. It's just this weird, bizarre mix of things that go on in that park. I was curious about the park, so I read that Jane Jacobs book — and it's interesting because she would consider this park really quite successful. Because there's so many things going on, there's not just one single thing. You see people walking their dogs and having picnics, and in the summer it's super fun because like the tightrope walkers are set up there, or they practise their fire thing, or you hear music, people are playing music, I love that. I love when there's busy-ness. I don't like quiet, that's why I live here. I like action. Ya gotta take a mix of everything. That's how I see it. So, I love the park actually, but there are certain things I don't like about it.

"When [my daughter] was little and I used to go to the park it was so great 'cause it was just across the street and so easy, and I'd meet friends there and that was nice. Like nothing really profound or anything, but it was just really nice to have the park … Mostly just hanging out in the park with my kid."

In the past, this woman didn't worry about her daughter being in the park without supervision. But now her daughter is a young woman, she feels differently. "[My daughter] is seventeen, and I am a parent, I worry. Now that she's older that I get more worried. I guess the drug thing. I don't want my kid to do drugs. Clearly! Which she doesn't. But, walking through the park as a pretty young woman is when comments, like that's more the worry. So yeah! So I would say I love the park and hate elements of the park at the same time."

Along with the worries about drugs and unsafe comments in the park, this woman spoke about violent incidents she and her family witnessed which often centred around the park. These experiences are part of her ambivalence towards the park and contribute to a general feeling of unease for her.

Frank

Frank (third from left) as a child in 1966 in Victoria Park. Also pictured are his father and godfather. This photo is embedded in a rock on the Southeast corner of Victoria Park. City of Vancouver archives, Reference code: VPK-S625-: CVA 392-859, photographer Eric Lindsay.

Frank's family is originally from Italy. His father moved the family to the Commercial Drive area, and in 1969 back to Italy. They returned to Canada again in the early 70s. Frank's father, godfather and the men in the Italian community spent a lot of time in the park in the 50s and 60s, and Frank did too.

"There used to be a bench where they used to play cards, and play bocce. I used to go to the store for the guys. Buy them cigarettes, pop, and they keep giving me the change, all the Italian guys. Keep the quarter. 'Cause they'd be playing bocce and they'd need cigarettes. [They would go to the park] when it wasn't raining for sure, but usually on weekends all the time. Everyone would just congregate there, meet, get together and play bocce. And smoke cigarettes, and wear their long coats and hats and talk about the old Italian days when they were in Italy, and how life was hard, how hard it was for them, being immigrants. Sort of where the guys hung out. I am sure they were looking for work, being new Canadians."

It was a social space for Frank's family and the broader Italian community. "It was like a park, just played. Go hang out, kick a soccer ball, and hang around and meet other kids, but back then it was just a simple park, with a few trees, no walkways, no nothing, just grass. When all the Italians immigrated here, where do you think they went? Commercial Drive! Odlum, McLean, Kitchener, Salsbury, that was the Italian community, that's where they all came. They came to Commercial Drive. That's where all the coffee shops are. And then they found a park … It [was] just a nice neighbourhood park, and it was so naive, the park, and it accepted all the Italians, and they're still going there! Like my godfather still goes there! They still hang around there, the ones that are still alive, yeah. If my dad was alive now he'd be going there too."

Frank thinks the park has changed, but he still sees it as a community park. "Well it has changed because it's now a dog park. It's got homeless people living in the park. And, you know, they drink in the park. It's now a neighbourhood park, it's for the community. For the children, they made a playground now. Back then there was no playground. Now it's used for dogs and the neighbourhood. And the residents. And the homeless. He [Frank's godfather] is a man of few words. He accepts everybody there. It's a diverse park now. Whereas before it was more bocce and cards and new Italians. Now it's a diverse area. It's Portuguese, everything. Brazilians, transients, it's just a different area. Nothing stays forever."

Frank has fond memories of the park from his childhood and is proud of having his photo embedded on the rock. "[I remember] my dad winning a bocce tournament! Yeah, it was nice. Yeah, him and his partner! They won the match and it was a good time and everyone's happy and smoking away their cigars and their cigarettes. Seeing my dad happy, being there, just the outdoors. After work they would show up there. On weekends they would go in the morning, spend all afternoon there, sometimes until sundown or until dinner time. A lot of history there. I am glad it's still there — the park. I feel like [the photo on the rock is] awesome. It's nice, it's nice to be a part of that history, nice to be a part of the archives."

Cease

Cease, the Indigenous Plant Diva, is a longtime resident of the Commercial Drive area and shared her thoughts on the park with me over tea at her kitchen table.

"Cease is literally my nickname. In Native communities, when you have your Native name, your non-Native name becomes your nickname. Cecilia is my full name, and then Cease is what everybody calls me, and then T'uy't'tanat is my traditional name. And it's from the Skwxwu7mesh Uxwumixw — the Squamish people, and t'uy't[1] are the plants, the medicines, and tanat is woman, so it could literally mean medicine woman, but more specifically means woman that travels by canoe to gather medicines for all peoples. So my life's work seems to be really collecting medicines as well as teaching people about medicines, and teaching people about the land that the medicines come from and how long they've been here. I am Skwxwu7mesh and Stó:lō. Those are my Coast Salish cultures, and so Skwxwu7mesh, the Skwxwu7mesh people, used this land here and this area known as East Vancouver."

Cease takes a broad perspective on the park. "When I look at parks, like Victoria Park, I think about how it's transformed and become this tiny green space and how it's a little tiny green dot left in an area that's not so green, but that is part of what's left of the interconnectedness of the original land and waters that were here.

"You look at parks in this area, all the ways they've morphed over time and changed and become the spaces they are now, and it's it is kind of a blip from the past that's left over, so we go back in time and we look at this area, and we erase all the streets and houses and go back 120 years, before there were streets here, before there were houses, and to think about the forest that was here. I walk a lot through Victoria Park, I've done plant walks through there with people, and we are putting things back, which is really good. Like, the rose hips, and other indigenous plants, ferns and such, that are all going back into the land to heal it and to re-indigenize it. And, that's something that people are doing in their yards too, even this yard has a lot of indigenous species in it, and you wander through this community and you start to see how people have gardened in the past. You can see a real story of the land, you see the stories of migrations, from many people. You see fig trees, plum trees, you see oaks, you see apple trees, that aren't from here, different fruit trees, and all these things tell a story of the last 120 years. Because everybody brought seeds from where they came from so they could plant them and have the things that meant everything to them.

"I've gone through there with people and had them just try to erase the society we see today just for a moment in time. I find when I am trying to connect to a piece of land, whether it is here in the city or go somewhere else to other people's traditional areas, I try to just find moments where I just stand on the earth and close my eyes and try to have a conversation with the land — whether it's holding on to a tree and just doing some breath work. It's a bit of a mindful moment thing. You're trying to connect to that piece of land and ask the land to tell you a story about itself and so I find it really helps. Even there in Victoria Park I've had people walk up and either hug the cedars and pines or just hold those trees for a moment and recognize their lives and how long those trees have been there and that they've been there 100–125 years, so they are still babies, but they're older than us and they've watched, they've witnessed, they've absorbed the stories of that neighbourhood. And so having a moment with those trees helps anybody that's trying to understand that neighbourhood, to ground in. It's like walking down the street every day, and you don't notice that elder always sitting on their porch but they notice you. And then one day you stop and talk to them and then they tell you stories you've never heard before.

"I look at this neighbourhood, from here, going down the slopes towards Clark Drive and beyond, and thinking about how this area was just a top of the saltwater marsh that used to flow up into the area where Clark Drive is now. This neighbourhood was just flowing with the animals and the people travelling through, so you have the three nations — the xʷməθkʷəẏəm, Tsleil-Waututh and the Skwxwu7mesh and then other Coast Salish tribes that are visiting and are travelling through and hunting. Elk were wandering through here and cougars and bears.

Just as my people and the other local nations were forced into smaller places, so were animals. We have always maintained our relationship with the wild natural world, and we still do today, We try to find ways to adapt to what's here, and even that little piece of green space is having to adapt to everything that's changed around it. So it's morphed from a natural little forest to having grass — which I see as an invasive species — it takes over, kills off indigenous plants, and it's really just there as luxury item to lounge on and sometimes just to look at. And when we think of how it looked before; it would have been a thick dense forest, and there probably wasn't any green, not a lot of green growing under there. The forest canopy wouldn't have allowed there to be grass, it would be a lot of decomposing elements of the deciduous and coniferous trees that grow in there. So, you know, cottonwood and the different fir trees and pine trees and cedar trees and yew, so all these different trees growing there, maybe Indian plum and maybe wild cherry. And so a lot of the food source has been taken away from there, now it is what it is. [Now it's] the same thing for non-Native people as it is for Native people. It's a place to go sit and leisurely hang out and enjoy the space, stop for a water break, or use the public washroom, hang out, watch activities in the park, read a book, whatever. Play in the playground with your kids.

It's a social space now but it doesn't mean it wasn't a social space before. It's a different kind of social space — it was a social space for animals and for Native people. We could have been hunting, we could have just been enjoying, we could have been meditating, doing just our time away from our people.

"Depending on the time of year, for us, all the uses of this area, like Victoria Park for instance, would be a fall and winter use, early spring. So whatever would be growing there, we would be gathering from there. We are looking for other shoots and things to start implementing into our diets, and thinking about the ways that we are going to eat and medicines we will drink and things we will do to get our body ready for the spring and summer and into the fall. So like this neighbourhood, it's really morphed in the last 120 years, but, you know, I feel like it hasn't totally lost its personality. I think the things that happen today are a reflection of the past. It's a social space now, for many cultures, but at one time, it was a social space for many species. Humans included. And whatever was there for us, to enjoy, whether it was relaxation, or gathering foods, it was there as a place to do the same thing we are doing today, which is a really good feeling.

"I have an opportunity with the things I do to always engage in the land and waters around here in ways that are not that different from my ancestors. I just have a cozier house with less people and really fancy appliances. I'm making all the things I need to make in an instant, and I'm working with the land, and I have a relationship with the land and the natural world that is so cut off today, and you know, so, it's a bit harder to have to build our community and have our relationship with the land. But it's like any time period for humans and animals — we have to adapt to what the times are and what the situations are and no matter what, I'm grateful that Victoria Park exists because it's still that green space and although for the most part the neighbourhood is really nice to walk through, it is nice to get away from all the houses that are right next to each other and just walk in a big open space and either walk on the path or the grass and just feel a bit more connected to T'shatamea, to mother earth.

"We are really lucky to have those green spaces, and I think it has a good personality, and I think, you know, the people that are there now, they're all from different places but probably guess that at least 70–80 percent of the people that frequent that park, especially the Italian community, that goes and plays lawn bowling, are all descendants, so many of their families have spent time there, and it's become their family zone, right?

"I've always, felt like it has a good energy. That's why I think it was always a social space, either for humans and/or animals and it kinda still is today as people walk their dogs through there. I am pretty sure neighbourhood cats at night are out there, hunting around and having fun and having their own little social network, and raccoons and coyotes. I always kind of chuckle when I go by 'cause I see so many things going on there. I'll see the lawn bowlers, people lounging, the occasional drunk person, people doing drugs deals and probably other deals, but I just get a chuckle out of it. I think it's great that this park can kind of have all these things going on, and then families playing [with] their little children or nannies watching people's kids, and people watching their dogs, some people hanging out, reading books and visiting, taking a break, a moment away from their hectic life. It's just a really positive public space, and I think parks are really, really important, which is why I did run for Parks Board. I was approached and asked if I would consider it. I said so without hesitation because of the fact I felt like if anybody is going to be in there, they should feel passionate about what the parks are, and of course I have my own Indigenous world view. I feel that Indigenous people should have more respect and rights to the land use across the city but I also think that for all citizens, if we are living here, we need to be neighbourly and use those public spaces together in a collective manner and respect one another. I should be responsible to the space that means something to me. I feel like everybody needs to have a more vested interest in our parks, and I always feel parks like Victoria Park are very loved by the community. People aren't just trashing it, they're not just there trying to be territorial, all those things are going on because people are feeling the energy that it is a common space. It's nice living in our little homes here but being outdoors is pretty special, and Vancouverites have it really good.

"I think about what the Indigenous people here have really had to sacrifice for others. We've sacrificed these public spaces, but we've sacrificed many public spaces, so when we have a small space like Victoria Park, or Grandview or Stanley Park, or Cates. Whatever those places are we have those, and we make the best use that we can out of them, and that's just what I hope for people in the 'hood. Is that they'll see that, and that's what I feel when I go by there."

Jacqui

Jacqui lived with her son Jamar on the park for sixteen years. She recently moved a few blocks away, but the park holds a very special place in her heart.

"I have amazing memories from the park. For me it's attached to Jamar and his growing up. We took advantage of just having a park as our backyard. All of our outdoor activities were at the park."

Jacqui loved the centrality of the park and the way it brought her family together with other people. "It was the hub of the neighbourhood. I always thought it was the perfect corner, being a block from everything and having this little park space because people didn't have yards to play in. I love the variety, how it just brought everybody together, every walk of life, and I got to see it." In the park, Jamar got the chance to play with neighbourhood kids, and Jacqui got the chance to meet new people, like the grandma of the kids next door. "I have this love for her. She would walk about the park every night. She said 'I always wanted to win the lottery so I could buy up the house next door and would move you in!' So cute, she was so nice. She was very caring, she was very sweet."

Later on, Jacqui and Jamar got a dog, and this meant Jacqui spent even more time in the park. "Then I got a dog, Abby, so it's like five times a day you're at the park, so you just, everyone you see who's there you see them every single day, and sometimes five times a day!"

One time, Jacqui had her camera stolen at the park, but that has been her only negative experience there. "I remember only one thing. I had a camera stolen, that was my one sort of sketchy experience, but it was my fault. I left it there, went and played baseball or something. But yeah that was one my moments. Do-over moments." Jacqui was never scared in the park. "I always felt safe even at night. I walk that park every single night, with the dog. Because there was always somebody around. It was never desolate. I feel sketchier and scared down by where we live now. I get all jumpy and I'm freaked out, whereas I was never scared in that park."

Overall, Jacqui feels very appreciative of the park. "It's so beautiful, and that light when it would come — you know that summer light — there was nothing more beautiful! There's all those trees I would just be in awe. I was just always so grateful that I had it. I never felt like I had the right to complain. People had noise complaints or [would complain about] the drinking, or people would call in and people were adamant about cleaning it up, but I just always thought no one was hurt, no one was offending me personally, I didn't feel unsafe, and I couldn't really hear the noise. I want it to be vibrant, and it doesn't have to be like picture cut-out perfect. I want the real issues, I want the realness of a neighbourhood, that's my preference. Not pristine and manicured, that's not my thing so maybe that's why I fit in perfectly! These are my people! I love that about it."

Jacqui is an elementary school teacher at a school in the area, and she likes running into families in the park. "I remember always seeing parents with little kids in the park and wondering if I was going to teach them one day. Over those years of meeting new families and seeing kids that I had taught was always fun. I love that. To me it's connection to your neighbourhood. I never wanted to teach out of the neighbourhood because I thought, these are my kids! I want to be connected, I want to know who they are, I want to teach the next generation, and the next sibling, because then I know the family. It's better for me."

Moving from the park was very hard for her, even though they got the opportunity to move into a good co-op apartment just a few blocks away. Jacqui says, "I got so emotional when I moved — I could cry now! And people thought I was crazy, because we got an opportunity to move into a co-op, which is just a gift. I guess I felt like I was leaving family and then leaving a corner of the hub of my universe. Everything to me was that corner. I just got so accustomed to having everything there, and I know change is good but I was so rooted. I hadn't been somewhere long-term in thirty years. I would live a year and move, or I would teach a year somewhere and then travel for a year. I'd never had roots, so when I had Jamar, I'm, like, okay this is my community, but it takes a long time to build that. It took years to feel like that's your community. It [moving] was traumatic."

I chatted with Tom when he was hanging out with a group of friends on the Victoria Drive side of the park.

Tom

"My name is Tom McGregor. Everybody knows me — around the Drive anyways. I actually stay on a porch right by Salsbury and First there. Right next to the church. It's only temporary. I don't know how long it's gonna be. I can't exactly say I grew up here 'cause I grew up in the system, like foster homes and running away on the street and stuff, but I always came back here. I used to go to Seymour Elementary, and I know all the parks around here, and this one especially"

Tom has lots of good memories in the park. "One time a long time ago, I was coming out of Grandview Church from an overnight, and it was morning time, and it was foggy, and there was a bunch of us, one of my best friends Noah, he's passed on now. It was foggy, and you couldn't see, like from here to there, right? We were all hanging out at the water fountain, having a drink, just getting out of the church, and an eagle flew right over us! It materialized out of the fog, and it flew right over us, and materialized back into the fog. That was amazing."

Victoria Park is one of Tom's favourite places to be. "I love the park. I don't know what to say about the park. I used to look around for roaches in this park, now I just buy it ... I drink in this park and I smoke marijuana. It's just like, marijuana park and it's not like a crack park or a whatever park, right, it's just like the hippie park! People are laid-back, oh and the Italians and the Mexicans, you know they're all cool too ... I like hanging out here it's nice and laid back compared to, like, Grandview Park, where everybody drinks so much and then everybody gets loud. This one's more like laid back."

The only thing Tom doesn't like about the park is the occasional police presence. He says "once in a while the cops come by and dump my booze, that's about it."

Tom works squeegeeing at an intersection close to the park, and goes back and forth many times a day. "So I can make like five bucks, quick five bucks, come out to the park, smoke a joint, go back, make enough for a bottle, you know, and, hang out in the park again. You know it's like two blocks away, something like that. Boom boom boom boom boom."

Tom gets along well with the other park goers. "We hang out over here, but just over there there's a whole bunch of kids and families and stuff. We kinda coexist ya know, and there's dogs ... so it's cool.

"I love it. I love the park. It's one of my favourite places to hang out in Vancouver. Salsbury Drive, Commercial Drive, this whole little area, in Vancouver, is where I live."

Tom passed away in December 2017.

Sunny bought his house by the park in 1991. He has done a lot of work to it and rents out the top two suites, living in the basement suite with his adopted daughter. He has seen the park and the neighbourhood change, getting less "wild" and more family-oriented.

Sunny

Showing me pictures of the progress of his renovations throughout the years, Sunny is clearly happy with his work. He shows me pictures of before, during and after his work, focusing on details that I would have never noticed. He also shows me pictures of the park. "I looked around, and this looked like an affordable place, and I work in construction, so I thought I can renovate it and rent it out. I did all the work myself, with my apprentice sometimes. It was quite a mess inside. I built all of this, all by myself! I was so proud of it. That's how the park looked, nothing much. You see, it's nothing. It's quite wild."

Sunny has seen the park and the neighbourhood change over time. "The park, they cleaned it up. Before, well they didn't have the playground. It was a little bit wild, and lots of drug users there. They would come to my house, I would find needles in the backyard, and even in my laundry room. They broke into my laundry room to use. In the old days I didn't like all the drug users. They are gone now."

Now, he sees the park as a community space and enjoys seeing children and families. "The bocce thing has always been there. That's a community thing, the Portuguese and Italian playing bocce. So they have a little pathway and put in benches, and the playground is very good for kids. There are lots young families here, moving in, lots of dogs and kids. I judge a neighbourhood by young kids, babies and dogs. My stepson, he came over with his two young daughters, and we played in the playground and we ran around, chasing each other. It's a family park."

Sunny uses the park quite a bit. "I play golf — so I used to take my golf club [and hit some balls in the park] and because the lawn was a little bit wild in the old days, I didn't care if I made some divots! But then, somebody warned me that, 'Hey there are kids playing around and you can hit them,' so I stopped doing that. In the summer, to cool down, I go take my little blanket and lie down under the trees. Oh, I like it very much. It's an open space for me to go and walk around. I don't like being cooped in. Sometimes, I have friends here and we sit on the bench and talk and it's that open-air feeling. They play music, and sometimes the people I know, they play, and it's great. I take my little fold up chair and go out there and listen. There's always music around the Drive somehow. People playing on the street. I hear the music so I go out."

Once, Sunny's adopted daughter was harassed walking home at night in the park. She came home crying, and Sunny went out with a sword [!] and threatened the men responsible. "So I said 'Don't you ever do that again, you have to answer to me,' to three of them, just scared. They didn't say anything. One of them said, 'Sorry, we had too much to drink.' Young guys. Hahaha."

"I grew up in a place called Maymyo in Burma. There's a beautiful park there. It's away from my house, and it's called Royal Lake. And we used to go there and play all the time. It's a little town of maybe 30–50,000 people. It's called a 'Hill Station' … The British government in Burma, and India, in the summertime it is very hot in the capital. So they go up in the hills, and move the government there. So they built houses, and they built the park. They used forced labour to build that park and they imported lots of fruit trees and plants."

Sunny first came to Vancouver in 1967. "First of all, the YMCA. First night. There I was roommates with a Canadian guy, from Hamilton, and we became friends. Then, my brother-in-law had a friend and he's got a room available, so I moved into his house in UBC. I lived there for maybe three or four months, then I found a place near City Hall. Just one room. From a friend I got to know from playing badminton. And I lived there for six months, and on and on and you know.

"I think I love this area. The local people, and you know, and when I go out, I always see somebody I know. It's really friendly, and I used to go to the Libra room to listen to music all the time, and from there I know lots of local people, and musicians, good musicians, and so that I would go out maybe four or five times a week, and see all the old friends. And one, the cook there, he called me the mayor of Commercial Drive!"

Ashley

Ashley has lived in East Van and around the park for most of her life. She has been a full-patch member of the Couture-Hern family for most of her life.

"I've babysat there. In the play area. I've just hung out in the grassy area, walked through, saw the bocce players. That park's kinda fun 'cause it's so distinct. There's the bocce area, then there's the grass area, and the kids area. It's a lovely park in general; its just a nice park. I have some nice memories there, like when we used to do the community kitchen thing. And it's always been a nice park even a long time ago it was nice."

Ashley used to babysit in the park and spent a lot of time in the play area. "Most of my memories are from taking Mika there. I used to babysit him every Monday, so we'd go to that park and then we'd walk to Britannia, so just playing there is like my fondest memory 'cause he was so little and amazing."

Near the bocce courts, Ashley often gets yelled at, so she avoids that area. "I guess with any park, anywhere in Vancouver there's sometimes people that aren't that lovely. The bocce men are not always the most polite men. In the bocce area, there's maybe a little mob mentality because they've all played there for so long and it's predominantly men, and as a young woman walking by they do the cat calling and whatever, which is shitty obviously, but it's definitely characteristic of it. One of the most vivid memories [in the park] is being yelled at by bocce guys. Like the majority of the time. In that zone. I stay in the other zones!"

As a teen, Ashley and her family moved to Port Hardy. When she moved back to Vancouver, she lived near the park. "I was just happy to be back. I've always loved East Van. I love East Van and I think that sometimes maybe what bugs other people about East Van are not things that have ever, like, bothered me in the sense that I don't feel safe, but I think some people think 'oh East Van it's not that great of a neighbour-hood' but I've never felt that way. I guess just 'cause it's home. A lot of the people I care about grew up in this neighbourhood. I love how mixed it is with its different cultures. I love that there's, like, such a variation of the things that you can do here, or the restaurants you can go to."

Ashley has funny memories in the park too. "I'm remembering a dinner we had in Victoria Park. We brought over a bunch of blankets. It must have been some occasion because there was a bunch of us together. And I think we got Indian food. Which is like — who brings Indian food to a park! It's the worst idea ever! So we were on the ground, there was no seats, we just put a blanket down and we had all this Indian food, and it was such a disaster, and I had hurt myself, and Matt's, like, you know — crippled! So like neither of us could get up off the ground after we ate the food! It was a funny time. Just lying down, eating Indian food in the park."

Clarence aka CD Dennis, Tsahaheh, May 2005. Photo credit: Ha-Shilth-Sa Newspaper.

Dave

Dave Dennis (Hiyu-kwiish-Miik) has lived on and off in East Vancouver all his life and is Nuu-chah-nulth – Sekani. Most recently he has worked as a housing organizer, property manager and project manager. He was one of the founders and spokesperson of the original West Coast Warrior Society and is a former president of the United Native Nations. In this interview Dave is speaking about his father, Whiskey Jack aka Clarence Dennis aka CD (pictured above), who passed away in 2017. CD spent a lot of time in the park.

"CD was in federal penitentiary for most of his young life, starting with boys reformatory. As a young man he robbed a few banks and ended up in federal penitentiary until he was thirty-two or thirty-three years old. Then he met my mom — I was conceived in prison, Cell Block H, I believe. When he got out he continued with his political activism and participated in Fred Quilt Committee and with the Union of BC Indian Chiefs.

"After my dad and I reconciled, he would follow from me from town to town, wherever I was living. In Nanaimo, after he had a falling out with his girlfriend, he decided to camp out. He'd go to the shelter and the soup kitchen occasionally, and he'd come by to visit but he wanted to be outside. After I got the job at UNN, he came to Vancouver as well.

"Back in the day the cops would harass homeless people with impunity. Every time the police would stop him and ask where he lived he would point all around him and say, 'I live here — under the sky.' Homelessness is so often considered a crime, and he was harassed all the time. He got beat up quite a few times by cops, white supremacists, racists.

"He was always very charismatic — people of all kinds always gravitated to him. He had what he called 'his hobo family' — they'd all hang out in McSpadden Park in the mornings because they'd sleep in the loading bays of the warehouses around there. In the mornings they would pool all their change: Growers Apple Cider was their favourite. They would always share everything communally. Most every day the cops would bust them up, so they would disperse and then they'd gather back at Grandview until they busted up again, and then they'd all head over to Bocce Ball Park most evenings.

"I think they all liked Bocce because it is not a major throughway, there's more room to chill. It's a bit more relaxed and out of the way. That was the park where they could chill and not get harassed.

"I felt okay with him sleeping out when I understood why he didn't want to be inside. At one point during his time in prison he was in the hole for more than nine months — administrative segregation they call it now — but really it is torture. Being confined in isolation like that fucks with your mind. Ever since then he didn't like the idea of being indoors for too long. We always offered to have him stay with us, or help him find a place. I found him an SRO place in the DTES one time, but he just said: 'I can't be down there son.' I worried lots of times when it was cold or wet — but it was his choice. He really wanted to be free outside. The Kettle Friendship Society was a great place for him — they have really good resources, people he really respected there — so any time he needed something he would head over there for a coffee and food and a dry place.

"In the beginning I had kind of a conservative attitude — I kept telling him, admonishing him to pull it together — but he didn't want to be downtown — he was too free. He never had ID and he resisted every time it felt like there was too many rules. Because of his time in residential school, because of his time in incarceration — he just wanted — needed — the freedom to be outside and go whenever and wherever. When I started to really understand him and his history, I began to understand why he wanted to live like that. He had this attitude — he knew that so many Indian people are out there suffering — and he didn't want to be any better than anyone else — if our people are suffering on the streets, he wanted to be there with them. He knew he could help them, not as a political organizer — but he was a mentor to so many people. He was always talking about being good to each other, how important it was for people to take care of each other. On the street, but everywhere.

"In residential school they used to do aptitude tests on the kids — all the while they were malnourishing them, and abusing them, and doing experiments on them. All over the west coast residential schools they would pick out kids who were at very advanced levels — and on his test he scored as a genius. He was an incredibly intelligent man. When he was in prison he started the Native Book Club and he would teach other prisoners how to read. He could have been an astrophysicist — he could pick up any book and just understand the whole thing — he could have been anything. One of his greatest joys was to go down to the Public Library and go through all the *National Geographics*, learn about people all over the world.

"He was such a gifted orator — most speakers end up talking all about themselves — but he would always look at an audience and say 'Look at all you beautiful people.' And it wasn't a con — it was genuine, he wanted our people to believe we are a beautiful people. I don't even want to call them speeches — he was just a good storyteller. Everywhere I'd go as a young activist, people would always recognize my facial structure, my gait, my style, and ask 'You CD's son?' People all over the province knew and respected him.

"I remember one time we had a big family gathering down at my Auntie's place. We were organizing a potlach and all my dad's brothers and sisters were there as well as all kinds of other family members. CD came wandered into this big crowd holding a bottle of Southern Comfort, and immediately he — and everyone else — noticed that two of his exes were there. It was a little tense for a minute, so he went over to a corner, sat in this comfortable chair, looked around, smiled and goes 'WHOooaaa!'

"He was always really a good-looking guy and I remember he used to look at me and say: 'This is how handsome you're going to be when you're 71!' Even now when I'm missing him and want to reflect on his life, if I go into Grandview Park or Bocce Ball Park, I'll find some of his people. And every time they recognize me and want to talk to me about him. It helps me remember that his spirit is everywhere and lives on."

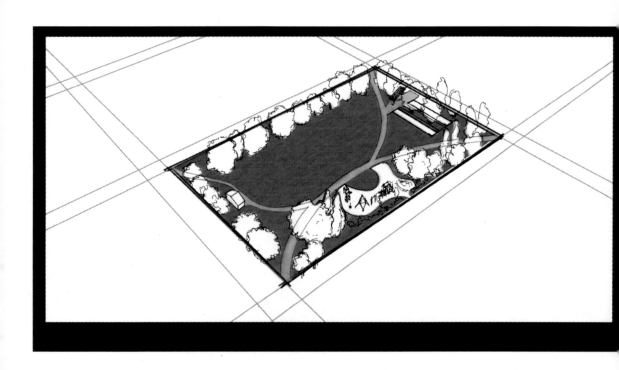

5

TITLING
VICTORIA PARK

I've just finished a research session at the Vancouver Public Library's Central Branch Special Collection, which holds a number of important books on the development of city parks. I'm ready to head home to East Van, but given all of the names of historical figures I've just been reading about, I'm going to ride a different route than usual. I hop on my bike and head four blocks northwest towards Vancouver's downtown core, stopping for a minute on Seymour Street, where I see the contrast of the iconic Hudson's Bay building (built in 1916) kitty-corner from the Telus Garden, which opened in 2015 as Canada's "most sustainable office building." Then I head northeast on Seymour for one block and join up with the Dunsmuir bike lane, which is a busy separated lane running through downtown and over the Viaduct — a leftover and soon to be dismantled part of a derailed highway system. Even though the bike lane is a great way to get in and out of downtown I'm not going to take the full route today because I'm aiming to find Keefer Street. I turn just before the Stadium Skytrain station and take a shortcut down some stairs (awkwardly carrying my bike) and come out onto Keefer Place. Riding along Keefer Ave, on my left is the Dr. Sun Yat-Sen Chinese Garden and Park as well as the Chinese Veterans Memorial with the "Zhong" character, meaning moderation and harmony, along with figures of a World War Two soldier and a railway worker. I've now passed Main Street, just two blocks south of Hastings & Main, which is the epicentre of the Downtown Eastside neighbourhood — infamous nationally as a place of drug-use and poverty. It is also a much loved and fiercely protected community, anchored by the Carnegie Community Centre on that same corner.

As I continue along Keefer, the neighbourhood changes into Strathcona — one of the oldest residential sections of the city. On my right is a large BC Housing low-rise complex, and on my left is the Mau Dan Garden Housing Co-op, built after the urban renewal plans of the 1960s had destroyed much of the residential housing in the area. Since I'm on my bike, I pass over the sidewalk and stop for a minute to get a drink from a public drinking fountain (which sits on top of a fire hydrant) on the west side of Maclean Park. On this sunny afternoon, the busy park is full of children (one of whom is wearing an amazing gold glitter bomber jacket riding their bike madly around the dry water park) and people playing sports or sitting against the baseball backdrop in lawn chairs they've pulled out, enjoying the sun after a long rainy winter. I keep riding along Keefer, which ends abruptly in two blocks at another BC Housing site, which abuts the railway tracks on its other side. I can see the Russian People's Hall to the right and the mural honouring the Indigenous Catholic saint Kateri Tekakwitha outside of the Sacred Heart Parish on my left. I turn left on Campbell even though it's slightly out of my way and head north across Hastings. I have to do a bit of dipsy-doodling, turning left and right, in order to get around the traffic control measures that regulate the flow in and out of downtown through this semi-industrial section of the Downtown Eastside. As I get closer to the Port of Vancouver, the security starts getting intense, but I can still appreciate the views of the North Shore mountains, the inlet and the oldest industrial site in Vancouver, the BC Sugar factory (built in 1890). Cautiously I make it onto Powell Street, and I join up with the recently created separated bike lane that I can follow east back to my neighbourhood. I ride along Powell to Clark Drive and turn south on this unfriendly-to-biking street and ride alongside six tractor trailers coming out of the port and heading south to the highways that lead to the interior. It's a bit of a dicey ride, and I eventually get off my bike and walk it across a few intersections in order to get to Odlum Drive. I ride along here for six blocks and come to Grant St. I rarely ride home this way because I've put myself at the bottom of a steep hill that I now climb in a very low gear up to Commercial Drive. Actually, I start to climb it and then decide — who am I kidding? — that walking would be better. It's a workout — and I'm sweating once I make it to the southwest corner

Victoria Park, day 362. Photo by Daisy Couture

of Bocce Ball Park. The late afternoon sun has come down under the cloud cover and the green grass is just beginning to glow. The weather is mild today, and I can smell a barbecue firing up.

It's taken me just a little over thirty minutes to get home along this slightly circuitous route — but in riding along these particular streets, I've also been riding along the streets named after the people who at one time held the property title to the land that became Victoria Park. In particular ways, these people were part of the way that settler relations to property ownership have been defined and constrained in this city. For most people who live on the east side of Vancouver, the names Seymour, Keefer, Heatley, Campbell, Powell and Odlum are familiar. They are the background to our daily lives and are repeated in such everyday and mundane ways that they have little meaning attached to them anymore — other than as a way to mark an address. Similar to the route I just rode home, I'm going to chart a path through the history of this small patch of grass that is now known officially as Victoria Park. It's a story intended to illuminate the settler colonial land theft that occurred here and Indigenous protection of land title that has been present all along. I hope this will go some way towards creating new understandings of the history that all of us who live in settler colonial lands share — and how we might work together to create a different future.

As we explained in the introduction to this book, Bocce Ball Park has been part of our family life since our early days in the city. We've decided to attend to the importance of the park — to us and to others — as a way to decipher the politics of occupied lands. My part of this work has been to look to the changing status of the land and how the place names that surround those of us who live on the east side of Vancouver are related to settler colonial land theft. As stated repeatedly by numerous Indigenous scholars, activists and leaders, decolonization is not a metaphor. Any work that purports to be engaged in decolonizing must be aimed at the return of Indigenous land and resources as well as the centring of Indigenous ways of knowing (Tuck and Yang 2012: 1). Engaging with the specifics of each nation's methods of self-governance as a settler is daunting. If colonial relations to land are extractive and aimed at creating profit without care for the impact on future generations while denying Indigenous peoples authority in their homelands, then non-colonial relations centre local Indigenous peoples' reciprocal relations with land, water and other-than-human beings. Yellowknives Dene political scientist Glen Coulthard describes this as *grounded normativity*, which refers to modes of "Indigenous land-connected practices and longstanding experiential knowledge that inform and structure our ethical engagements with the world and our relationships with human and nonhuman others over time" (2012: 13). The history of this land from 1864 to the present day includes actions by multiple Indigenous peoples throughout the province, and each group has their own relations to methods of governance. As a settler I do not have access to all of these ways of knowing. Instead I aim to have the descriptions of actions demonstrate Indigenous thought-ways as they contend with land theft. I am informed here by a local way of conceptualizing a visitor in an Indigenous language of the Lower Mainland. A visitor is understood as one who walks alongside. This guides my conception on how to behave — *walking*, a continual movement and present engagement with land that has minimal long-term impact, and *alongside* — in relation to the people who are already present who are also in motion. I am struck by the difference between the watching "by*stander*" that Carter describes in the quote with which we opened our book and the one who walks alongside. While walking with someone, you would have to be oblivious and uncaring not to share in their burdens.

I also spend a lot time thinking about the ways that theatre and performance effect change in the world, so I'm curious about ways that embodied actions and speeches that happen in public spaces might be one way into a different futurity. I am always intrigued by the radical German theatre artist and theorist Bertolt Brecht's work, which aims to defamiliarize situations, to "make strange" something that is taken for granted so that it might be seen as changeable and not inevitable. Brecht advocated myriad methods of creating a subjunctive mode in theatrical productions, where theatre artists perform in ways that create what he called a "not… but…" that would keep other possibilities present (1936: 114-15). This chapter takes up a stance of examining the world around us in East Vancouver, while also keeping present an idea of *not* property, *but* Indigenous land, with the aim to make strange settler presumptions of land title and Victoria Park as a step towards different relations to land.

I began this research on how the city created Victoria Park by tracing the changing legal status of the land.[1] I quickly found that the City of Vancouver purchased it from Adele Ann Seymour in 1909. I thought it was interesting that the seller was a woman, so I expanded the search, trying to figure out who she was, why she held title to the land and why she would have been willing to sell it to the city. As I traced the change in land title after the initial Crown grant to Edward Davis Heatley and George Campbell in 1872 to Seymour's sale to the city in 1909, the context of Indigenous resistance to settler encroachment throughout the province and locally became clear to me. That narrative helped me to historicize the land that became the park and the process through which city dwellers continue to feel entitled to this unceded land for their use and pleasure. I also couldn't help but find some private meaning in the mainly trivial fact that Adele Amy Seymour took possession of the land title one hundred years to the day that our daughter Sadie was born. It's a coincidence, but one that reminds me of the implications of living and raising our kids here.

To place the history of Victoria Park, I want to highlight a pivotal moment in the relationship between the Canadian settler state and Indigenous people west of the Rocky Mountains. On July 20, 1871, British Columbia joined Confederation, becoming the sixth province in the Dominion of Canada. This fact is taught to all Canadian school-children, although growing up in eastern Canada, the date didn't seem as important to me as the 1867 event in Charlottetown that is commemor-ated as the birth of the nation state. In BC, however, as I now understand, joining Confederation (deeply connected to Sir John A. MacDonald's promise to build a national railway) was seen by some to shift the land from that of a colony (and therefore subject to the Royal Proclamation of 1763) to part of the Dominion created by the British North America Act of 1867, whereby all land not owned by private individuals became Crown land. This slippage of Indigenous lands into Crown lands was controversial at the time, and the Dominion government first rejected the BC Land Act of 1874 on the grounds that it did not recognize Indigenous land title or include a process of treaty negotiation, as had been carried out throughout much of eastern Canada (Harris 2002: 92).

The refusal to engage with the Royal Proclamation and treaty negotia-tion protocols in BC is a significant part of the complex relations between contemporary settler colonial governance structures and Indigenous lands.[2] Indeed, after a visit to Vancouver Island in the summer of 1876, Governor General Lord Dufferin stated in a departing speech that the situation of the Indian land question in BC was unsatisfactory because the province had not recognized Indigenous land title since Governor James Douglas's time and that it had always been recognized in Canada. He was crystal clear about the process: "Before we touch an acre we make a treaty with the chiefs representing the band we are dealing with ... not until then do we consider that we are entitled to deal with an acre" (quoted in Harris 2002: 92). Dufferin also explained that by giving out grazing leases and alienating land from Indigenous people the province was interfering with "the prescriptive rights of the Queen's Indian subjects." The Dominion and provincial governments eventually agreed upon a commission that would decide on the size of reserves for Indigenous people, and somehow that process — which did not include an engagement with land title — was allowed to proceed by the Dominion government over the objections of the federal minister of justice (96–7).

This is what is meant when people state that the land in BC is "unceded." It was not purchased, nor was a treaty negotiated nor a war fought that would change the status of the land. This is an essential part of understanding BC's entry into Confederation and how the Western legal standards, beginning from the time that Canada was considered a British colonial holding, have not been followed. It is not surprising, therefore, that Indigenous organizing and resistance to this land theft has been continuous since the time of European settlement, and intensified after BC joined Confederation. It is also an incredibly difficult fact to wrap my head around as a settler raised in a capitalist society that holds private property as sacrosanct. How could it be that all of the property ownership in places not covered by treaty is illegitimate *by Western legal standards*, not to mention Indigenous conceptions of land relations? Looking out at the houses surrounding the park and the people happily going about their days carrying groceries home or picking up their dog's poo in the park, it seems impossible that we all just carry on, oblivious to the precarity of this situation.

Now that this rupture is clear, we need to go back to a time (in the decades before BC joined Confederation) when it seemed like another way might have been possible. In 1851, James Douglas (1803–1877), a former Hudson's Bay Company (HBC) official, was appointed the first governor of Vancouver Island. He was of Scottish and "free coloured" West Indian ancestry and he was married to Amelia Connolly, the daughter of a Cree woman, Susann Pas-du-nom, and William Connolly, Douglas's HBC superior. He began his leadership by recommending that the HBC purchase land from Indigenous people, and between 1851 and 1854, he negotiated fourteen "Douglas Treaties" — covering three hundred and fifty-eight square miles of Vancouver Island — with various Coast Salish groups and two Kwakwaka'wakw groups (Ray 2016: 182–93). Douglas also responded to tensions caused by the gold rush by creating reserved lands for Indigenous people, demarcated by Indigenous leaders themselves, which included village sites, burial grounds, potato patches and other "provisioning" areas. He also granted Lower Fraser Indigenous people the right to pre-empt land (Thor Carlson 2010: 168–73).

When Douglas retired in 1864, there was uncertainty regarding how his successors would handle Indigenous land reserves — and the incursion of white settlers into Indigenous lands was heightening tensions. During the Tsilhqot'in War of late April 1864, several road workers were killed, and eventually six Tsilhqot'in leaders, who had been invited to negotiate peace with colonial authorities, were instead arrested and executed for murder (these men were officially pardoned on March 26, 2018, by Prime Minister Justin Trudeau).

When Frederick Seymour (1820–1869), Douglas's successor as governor, received word of these attacks on May 14, 1864, he sent forces to put down the insurrection and then returned to his plan to establish good relations with Coast Salish people of the lower river area by inviting them to celebrate Queen Victoria's birthday on May 24. Between three to six thousand Indigenous people attended the event to honour the queen and show their appreciation for the large reserves just created in the Fraser Valley, according to Douglas's policy. They also requested compensation for the lands on which white people had settled (Thor Carlson 2010: 217–28). For the next ten years, the May 24 gathering was an annual event that was held up as an example of the loyalty Indigenous people had for the colonial government, as well as an opportunity for settlers to exoticize Indigenous people' dances and music.

However, the political intent behind the Indigenous people' involvement in these gatherings can be understood differently. Oral traditions circulating among two dozen contemporary Stó:lō families state that during the 1864 gathering, Seymour "agreed to a compensation formula that would see one-third of all revenues raised through the alienation of land outside of Indian reserves returned to the Stó:lō, the other two thirds to be divided equally between the federal and provincial governments" (Thor Carlson 2005: 3). Seymour Street, which runs through downtown Vancouver, is named in honour of this Frederick Seymour, who used his short time as governor of the mainland colony to promote British ideas of progress and economic

BC Archives. Reference code: A-03345, photographer, Richard Maynard, 1872

development. His efforts to keep friendly relations with Indigenous people were part of this goal.

The possibility of influencing the governor kept the May 24 gathering going until 1874, even after the reduction of the reserves in 1867. At the last gathering, Indigenous leaders presented the new governor (Joseph Trutch) with a petition that listed their concerns as well as their ideas regarding just options for redress. Their proposal included 80 acres of land per nuclear family and ended with a statement that if these things weren't addressed, there would be ill feelings and uncertain consequences (Thor Carlson 2010: 233). When, in mid-May 1875, the government still hadn't responded to their concerns, they cancelled their participation in the gathering entirely. Clearly, for those Indigenous people, the

Province
~~Colony~~ of
BRITISH COLUMBIA.

Victoria by the Grace of God of the United Kingdom of Great Britain and Ireland and of the Colonies and Dependencies thereof in Europe Asia Africa America and Australasia **Queen** Defender of the Faith and so forth **To all to** whom these presents shall come **Greeting**

KNOW YE that WE do by these presents for US Our Heirs and Successors in consideration of the sum of *One Thousand two hundred and one dollars and eight Cents* to US paid give and grant unto *Edward Davis Heatley and George Campbell as tenants in Common* their heirs and assigns all that parcel or Lot of Land situate *in New Westminster District British Columbia* said to contain *One Thousand two hundred and one acres* more or less and numbered *Lot Two hundred and sixtyfour (264) group One (1)* on the Official Plan or Survey of the said *New Westminster District* ~~Province~~ in the ~~Colony~~ of British Columbia to Have and To Hold the said parcel or Lot of Land and all and singular the premises hereby granted with their appurtenances unto the said *Edward Davis Heatley and George Campbell as tenants in Common* their heirs and assigns for ever

PROVIDED NEVERTHELESS that it shall at all times be lawful for US our Heirs and Successors or for any person or persons acting in that behalf by OUR or their authority to resume any part of the said lands which it may be deemed necessary to resume for making roads canals bridges towing paths or other works of public utility or convenience so nevertheless that the lands so to be resumed shall not exceed one-twentieth part of the whole of the lands aforesaid and that no such resumption shall be made of any lands on which any buildings may have been erected or which may be in use as gardens or otherwise for the more convenient occupation of any such buildings

PROVIDED NEVERTHELESS that it shall at all times be lawful for US Our Heirs and Successors or for any person or persons acting under OUR or their authority to enter into and upon any part of the said lands and to raise and get thereout any gold or silver ore which may be thereupon or thereunder situate and to use and enjoy any and every part of the same land and of the easements and privileges thereto belonging for the purpose of such raising and getting and every other purpose connected therewith paying in respect of such raising and getting and use reasonable compensation

PROVIDED NEVERTHELESS that it shall be lawful for any person duly authorized in that behalf by US Our Heirs and Successors to take and occupy such water privileges and to have and enjoy such rights of carrying water over through or under any parts of the hereditaments hereby granted as may reasonably required for mining purposes in the vicinity of the said hereditaments paying therefor a reasonable compensation to the aforesaid *Edward Davis Heatley and George Campbell as tenants in Common* their heirs or assigns.

In testimony whereof We have caused these Our Letters to be made patent and the Great Seal of ~~Our Colony~~ of British Columbia to be hereunto affixed Witness OUR right trusty and well-beloved *Joseph William Trutch* Lieut Governor ~~and Commander-in-Chief~~ of ~~OUR Colony~~ of British Columbia and its Dependencies at OUR Government House in OUR City of Victoria this *twentyeighth* day of *June* in the year of Our Lord One thousand eight hundred and *Seventy two* and in the Thirty *Second* year of OUR Reign.

By Command

Campbell and Heatley's Crown Grant. BC Crown Land Registry GATOR

gatherings were politically positioning a nation-to-nation relationship with the Crown, as per the Royal Proclamation of 1763. We also see this positioning in the 1872 gathering — the year following BC's entry into Canadian confederation — where the public event took the form of a rally held at the Land Registry Office in New Westminster (see photo pg. 121) to protest the disregard of Indigenous title that was part of BC's new status as a province (Tennant 1990: 53).

I focus on the New Westminster gathering because I see it (and the relations around colonial land policies that are represented through it) as intimately connected to our small patch of grass here in East Vancouver. The initial Crown grant that gave property title of the land that would become most of the east side of Vancouver (including Victoria Park) to Europeans is dated June 26, 1872, about a month after that event. The grant of land would not have been possible had the new province been following legal precedent throughout the rest of Canada. This is the first layer placed over this piece of land that changed its status. I wonder what would happen if I printed out and laminated the Crown grant and put it up in the park. Would anyone understand its significance? Would it be a source of pride for local settler historians who celebrate the "heritage" of this neighbourhood?

The province was still so new that the Crown grant form still refers to British Columbia as a colony, with that word crossed out and "province" handwritten over top. The signature on the document is Joseph William Trutch's, named as the queen's "right trusty and well-beloved Lieutenant Governor." Trutch (1826–1904) was an Englishman who came to BC in 1859 during the Fraser River gold rush after working as a surveyor on the west coast of the United States and speculating on land in the Midwest for the previous ten years. He began his career in BC as a contract engineer and surveyor for the government, working in the Fraser River and Canyon area. Through his surveying contracts he was able to learn where the most desirable land was and bought large holdings, especially on Vancouver Island, where he was elected as a member of the House of Assembly in 1861. In 1864, the outgoing governor of BC, James Douglas, named him Chief Commissioner of Land and Works, despite public outcry over his conflict of interest due to his own land-holdings and extensive government contract work. When Douglas retired, Trutch, working under Governor Seymour, refused to recognize Indigenous title. He reduced the size of the reserves Douglas had set out by 92 percent, mischaracterizing those reserves as made through the "improper activities of a rogue surveyor operating under dubious instructions from an aging and anachronistic governor" (Thor Carlson 2010: 173). After the gold rush ended and the colony faced economic hardship, Trutch advocated joining with Canada. When BC became a province, he was appointed lieutenant governor, serving from 1871 to 1876, and was then appointed as Dominion agent to BC responsible for railway issues, serving until 1889, whereupon he was knighted for his service.

It was early on during his term as lieutenant governor that Trutch signed Campbell and Heatley's Crown grant, although given the extensive conflicts of interest between his business dealings and his government offices, as well as his dismantling of Douglas's reserves, it is now clear that he was not as "right trusty" as the Crown may have believed. Campbell and Heatley, who were partners in the Hastings Mill, bought the land for $1/acre. Edward Davis Heatley was based in San Francisco and George Campbell oversaw the mill's workings from Victoria. They prospered as the owners of the mill from 1870 to 1889 (Snyders and O'Rourke 2000: 54; Underwood 2010: 35). Their Crown grant (as was standard) stipulated that the Crown reserved the right to resume title of up to one-twentieth of the land if needed for public works (although land that had buildings or gardens on it would be exempt). The second and third clauses clarified that the Crown reserved the right to any gold or silver found on the land, as well as any water that might be necessary for mining activities.

Essentially, they were granted title for the top layer of the land, which wouldn't have been a problem for Campbell and Heatley, as they were likely most interested in the lumber from the forested lands adjacent to their mill. The purchase may also have been part of a speculation on how the property value would increase once the railway made it to the coast. These clauses in the grant also fit in well with the contemporary analysis of Sylvia McAdam (Saysewahum), a Nêhiyaw (Cree) woman and cofounder of the Idle No More movement in the winter of 2012, who explains that her continuing work to defend the forests on her land is a necessary first line of defence against mining and water resource development. Heatley and Campbell cleared the lands they bought, starting at the higher ground and rolling or dragging the trees downhill to the shore, where the mill was located. As Victoria Park is near the top of this high ground (in what has become known as the Grandview neighbourhood), the area would have been the first to be logged. That steep hill I walked my bike up from Odlum Drive was a great way to get the lumber to the shore in those days. Their clearing of this land made possible the "grand view" of the mountains and lower lying areas, which contributes to the pleasure of living and walking around this neighbourhood.

Once the logging was complete and the railway was well on its way, the land prices began to soar. With the railway route finally set in 1881, after the southern route through the Rockies was found, land speculation on the west coast began in earnest. The announcement that the Canadian Pacific Railway terminus station would be near Coal Harbour (instead of Port Moody as had been thought) was delayed until January 14, 1885, in order to ostensibly mitigate speculative real estate purchases in the Granville townsite area (now Vancouver). Included in the deal to relocate the terminus was a provincial land grant of 6,000 acres (MacDonald 1977: 7–12). On February 24, 1885, Campbell and Heatley sold 160 acres of their DL264A lots, for the same $1/ acre price that they had paid for them, to Dr. Israel Wood Powell (1836–1915), on his way to becoming the fifth-largest landowner in the city by 1887.[3] While this all sounds like normal land dealings between business owners of the time, it was controversial.

Real estate agent W.E. Graveley recounted to Vancouver archivist J.S. Matthews in 1932 that Powell's purchase of the lands was part of a land syndicate created through an early tip about the Coal Harbour terminus station from a CPR official to A.W. Ross (Matthews 207-08, 252). The men involved in the land-buying group included the Oppenheimer brothers, the Keefer brothers, Powell and ten others. On May 16, 1885, a few months after Powell completed this purchase, the *Port Moody Gazette* printed their names as a way to expose the unfair dealing. The press exposure had little effect on the dealings of these powerful men, who continued to profit from their position in a network of privilege. This is just one more way of understanding how land speculation is embedded in the DNA of Vancouver and is a local settler tradition and not, as is often touted in reactionary media, a threat from "foreign" buyers..

While these federal and provincial activities regarding a transcontinental rail system and the trade in land titles were going on, Indigenous people continued to refuse to accept the theft of their unceded land, which legally still belonged to them; settlers had no right to buy and sell this land. In 1881, the Nisga'a sent a delegation to Victoria to demand recognition of their title. When this was not satisfactory, the Tsimshian sent delegates to Ottawa in 1886. The following year the two groups sent a joint party of chiefs to Victoria to demand an inquiry into title and self-governance issues and to ask for treaty negotiations (Ray 2016: 320). Since repeated efforts over the previous years had achieved no tangible results, this delegation "requested verbatim transcripts be made of the meeting and that printed copies be sent to the Indians afterwards"; apparently they had little trust in anything government officials might say. They demanded an immediate public inquiry into the land issue, which demonstrates that they still had some belief that a process of public discussion could resolve the situation. The Victoria meeting members included Tsimshian and Nisga'a representatives as well as the premier, attorney-general and Indian Commissioner Israel Wood Powell (Tennant 1990: 55–65). No treaty commission was established, but the province sent a two-person joint federal-provincial commission to hold a hearing about disputes over land between settlers and Indigenous people, with explicit instructions to make no promises concerning title (Ray 2016: 320).

Representing the Dominion at that 1887 Victoria meeting was the same man, Dr. Israel Wood Powell, who purchased the lands from Campbell and Heatley in 1885. Besides being a large landowner, he was also a medical doctor and a major politician in the years before BC joined Confederation. Powell, who was from Upper Canada originally, arrived on the west coast in 1862 following the Cariboo gold rush and was elected to the House of Assembly on Vancouver Island shortly after his arrival. He advocated for BC's entry into Confederation and was appointed the federal superintendent of Indian affairs, as well as the lieutenant-colonel of the militia (in the event that there needed to be military force in dealings with Indigenous people). Powell exerted pressure on the provincial government to establish land reserves for Indigenous people that could serve as adequate economic bases.

It is important to understand that while reserved lands were nominally being set aside by colonial governments as a way to protect Indigenous people from settler encroachment, they also had the result of keeping people in place for easier monitoring by Indian agents. The policy on reserves shifted away from their use as an economic base, close to traditional territories, to eventually being a minimal area given for Indigenous use until their complete assimilation no longer required them. In keeping with Powell's assimilationist goals, he supported boarding schools for Indigenous children, and soon after becoming superintendent also began pressuring the federal government to ban the "potlatch" because these ceremonies were understood as a way that elders could pass on their traditional values and influence the younger generations (Ray 2016: 224). Prime Minister John A. Macdonald issued an order-in-council on July 7, 1883, for Indigenous people to abandon "potlatching" and followed it up with an amendment to the Indian Act on April 19, 1884, that made it a misdemeanor to participate in a "potlatch" or a "Tamanawas" dance, subject to imprisonment for a minimum of two months and a maximum of six.

While federal law may have restricted these Indigenous governmental performative systems, it did not prevent Indigenous people from engaging in their ceremonies. For example, in 1888, after a magistrate from Hazleton told the Gitxsan people in Kitwangak to stop potlatching, their leader replied that the "law was a weak baby" and defied both the magistrate and the government. Initially, the province of BC did not support the federal law, refusing to send police to back up Indian agents who tried to enforce it or allow the use of their jails until 1889 (Ray 2016: 226–27). Powell's work to ban the "potlatch" as a method to interrupt cultural influences and hasten assimilation also had the effect of interrupting Indigenous methods of establishing and transferring rights to land and resources. What colonial administrators called the "potlatch" was actually multiple ceremonies which were part of the governing and legal system, creating witnesses to changes in status (such as marriages and naming), which themselves carried privileges to resources.

These practices had expanded in the early years of contact with Europeans as many interactions had created new economic prosperity, and also epidemics of disease spread by newcomers caused social disruptions necessitating ceremonial activities to re-establish order. So, while Powell's work to assure a reasonably sized reserve base may have been enlightened for his time, his efforts to eliminate ceremonial practices undermined Indigenous methods of recognizing title to lands within their own governing systems. Despite the 1884 ban, the practices continued, although they were necessarily smaller and held in more remote areas to avoid the RCMP and Indian agents, thus limiting Indigenous people' ability to create large numbers of witnesses. This section of the Indian Act was not repealed until 1951.

Powell's efforts to create boundaried areas for Indigenous people and to disrupt their methods of transferring resource rights helped to create the imaginary province that was promoted by pamphlets such as one published in 1886 by the federal Department of Agriculture in Ottawa entitled "Province of British Columbia. Information for Intending Settlers, with a map." Stamped on the cover in red ink are the words: "Be sure your ticket reads Canadian Pacific Railway to Insure Satisfaction," demonstrating a clear link between the government and the company. The pamphlet opens with an argument about why BC is better than California, Washington or Oregon in terms of the quality of the wheat, barley, hops, beef and mutton. The authors assert that the province has more and better coal than anywhere else, as well as "fine harbours, superior fish, sounder trees." Settlers are also assured of easy access to land: "The public domain is sold cheaply, the taxation is immensely less, titles are more secure" and that in terms of its climate, harbours and resources, BC "may be regarded as, in many respects, a duplicate in North-West America, of Great Britain and Ireland." Powell's influence on the treatment of Indigenous peoples, from education, reserved lands and the disruption of cultural practices (combined with his use of his privileged position in government to speculate on lands surrounding the CPR terminal) make him particularly poignant symbol of the multiple ways Indigenous lands and cultures were under assault during the late nineteenth century. His legacy does not go unmarked — remember my bike ride along Powell Street? The street name commemorates his work in BC, but needs an expanded understanding of how weighty this inheritance should be.

Nearly three years after the Indian Act amendment banning the "potlatch," on November 14, 1887, Powell sold part of his holdings to George Alexander Keefer (a co-member of the land syndicate); this was six months after the first CPR train had arrived in the city. Keefer (1836–1912) came to the coast as a contractor with CPR and immediately began work to establish the Vancouver Water Works and Electric Illuminating Companies. His companies won the contracts to install electric lighting in the city, to bring water from the Capilano River across the inlet at the First Narrows and to run electric trams, all by 1890, thus creating the civic infrastructure necessary to modern city life. The transit and electric companies he co-owned amalgamated into the Vancouver Electric Railway and Light Company, which eventually became BC Hydro (Snyders and O'Rourke 2000: 150). His name is preserved in the street that runs through Chinatown and Strathcona, two of the oldest neighbourhoods of the city, neighbourhoods replete with small businesses, subsidized provincial housing, community halls and at least one church. While his early work created the pipes and wires that are the backbone of a city and he profited from his inclusion in a land speculation syndicate, the street with his name on it now has the kinds of social infrastructure that makes living in one of the most expensive cities in the world possible for lower income people.

Keefer kept the land for just over two years, selling all of Block 137 (about 140 lots, situated in the six city blocks enclosed between the Commercial Drive, First Avenue, Victoria Drive and Kitchener Street) to three men — John F. Van Horne, John H. Stafford and Wheeler Greens — on December 2, 1889. These names do not show up as street names in East Vancouver as all the previous owners of the land do. The only reference to them I found was a city clerk's notice published for the week of June 11–19, 1902, in the *Vancouver Daily Mail*, that two of their jointly held properties, totaling twenty lots in DL264a, were sold for back taxes totaling $278.55 (these lots are located along Grant Street between Commercial and Victoria). The men's names are included in a list of over four hundred properties of various sizes sold off by the city at auctions earlier in the year, some for as little as $5 (*Vancouver Daily World* 1902). The timing of their land purchase, a few years after the boom caused by the completion of the railway, likely made good financial sense at the time, but the ensuing depression in the mid to late 1890s halted the growth of the city. By 1893, about half the bricklayers in the city had no work, nor did two-thirds of the carpenters. In 1896, Mayor Henry Collins declared personal bankruptcy, and tax revenues dropped significantly (Macdonald 1977: 31). The sale of land for unpaid taxes during this economic downturn is a good reminder that dealing in property can be risky — particularly for people who do not travel in powerful circles of privilege. Van Horne, Stafford and Greens did manage to sell part of their land holdings before the depression hit, including the site of the future Victoria Park, to Malcolm Matheson on September 13, 1890.[4] Matheson sold it to Adele Ann Seymour on January 18, 1892.

Adele Seymour [nee Adams] was from Goderich, Ontario, and moved to Vancouver in 1892, after marrying her husband, Joseph Richard Seymour (1858–1933), in St. Catharines. He was a small businessman, pharmacist, real estate developer and leader in the Scottish Rite Masonry fraternal order. The Seymours had four children, Murton, Ansley, Ruby and Adele, and lived on Robson Street. As far as I can tell, they were not related to the earlier colonial governor Frederick Seymour.

They were personal friends and later neighbours of Vancouver's first city archivist, James Skitt Matthews. Matthews kept a file on the family, detailing the achievements of their sons during World War One, Adele's misadventures with Skunk Cabbage flowers when she first moved to the coast, and their daughter's donation of the family collection of "Indian and Australian relics" to the city museum. Matthews also includes details about Mr. Seymour's drugstore business, the location of the stores and the rents he paid, and that he sold them to a larger firm in 1902 for $25,000. Besides his work as a druggist, Seymour also started a real estate business, Seymour, Marshall, Storey and Blair, speculating on property, including one failed effort to develop vacation homes in North Vancouver. Also included in Matthews' file is a pamphlet, "Joseph Richard Seymour: Founder of Scottish Rite Masonry and Royal Order of Scotland in British Columbia," published by the Canadian Masonic Research Association in 1967. The fullness of Seymour's involvement in the public life of the city is detailed here. He served as president of Hudson's Bay Mortgage Corp. of Vancouver, was vice-president of North American Building and Loan Co., treasurer of Vancouver branch of Red Cross during the Boer War — and then vice-president at outbreak of WWI. He organized

The Seymour's fiftieth wedding anniversary in J.S. Matthews' backyard, 1933. City of Vancouver Archives. Reference code: AM54-S4-: Port N134.1, photographer, J.S. Matthews

the Canadian Red Cross Association for mainland BC during the war and promoted Victory Loans connected to the Patriotic Fund. He later became superintendent for Vancouver Docks, held the position until his death in 1933 and was the president of the BC Conservative Association. He also helped establish the Anglican Theological College and served as chair of Vancouver School Board (Greer 1967: 1–3). The pamphlet describes him as the best known and most respected Mason in BC.[5] It is unclear from the historical documents why Adele Seymour held the title to the land instead of her husband, and how she came to purchase it on January 18, 1892, as the biography of her husband states that the family moved to Vancouver permanently in November of that year. As a married woman, she had had the right to own and administer her own property since the early 1870s in various places across Canada, including BC in 1873; therefore, this purchase could have been her own investment as her family moved to the west coast (Falcon 1991: 27). The importance of her married status is emphasized in the title documents, which list her name as registered owner and then in brackets afterwards "wife of J.R. Seymour." We do know that she held title throughout the depression of the 1890s and through most of the first decade of 1900. As there is an image of the family home on the 1000 block of Robson St. dated tentatively from 1893 in the archives, the purchase of this land may have been an early part of their efforts to establish a real estate business or purchase land as an investment.

Throughout the seventeen years that Adele Seymour held the title to the square block that is now Victoria Park, the population of the city grew from approximately 15,000 people to almost 80,000 ("City of Vancouver Population"). The growing settler population continued to buy and sell land title while local Indigenous people continued to assert their rights and expectation for compensation for the taking of their lands. One key event, which probably went little noticed by the settlers of the Lower Mainland, was the 1898 approval of an order-in-council by the federal cabinet to extend Treaty 8 into northeastern BC, laying out reserves from land previously turned over for railway and agricultural usage — 640 acres per five-person family. The federal government then spent seventeen years trying to meet with various groups to ensure they adhered to the treaty — but this work was never completed. This northern BC treaty is significant to ongoing land title struggles because the province did not object to the treaty and it "stands as irrefutable evidence that aboriginal title was recognized in a good portion of British Columbia and that the principles and procedures set out in the Proclamation of 1763 could be applied to Indians and Indian lands in the province" (Tennant 1990: 65–67). So, although the provincial officials convinced the Dominion to overlook the necessity of treaty negotiations when BC joined Confederation in the 1870s, adhering to Treaty 8 in BC territory demonstrates that both the federal and provincial governments recognized Indigenous title and that treaties were necessary to secure access to land and resources. This was all very far from the Lower Mainland however, and did not cause a ripple in settler conceptions of their right to buy and sell property. As it flew in the face of provincial policy with regard to Indigenous land title, when the federal officials requested approval from the BC government for this treaty, this was ignored (Ray 1999: 38).

Locally, a leader from the Squamish Nation, Su-á-pu-luck/Chief Joe Capilano, began organizing a delegation of Indigenous people to bypass the provincial and federal governments, and discuss the problem of land title with King Edward VII himself. Su-á-pu-luck/Capilano was an effective organizer who travelled throughout the province, speaking in Chinook jargon[6] to the assembled Indigenous people, so that, while provincial officials and journalists knew he was organizing something, they were unaware of the details. In fact, when the delegation to the king paraded to the train station in 1906, the mayor's office sent representatives to wish them well on their journey (Thor Carlson 2005: 11–12). An important outcome of the trip to London was that Su-á-pu-luck/ Capilano met Tekahionwake/Pauline Johnson (1861–1913) while she was performing there. Tekahionwake/Johnson was an internationally acclaimed poet of Mohawk and English heritage. She was an active writer and performer throughout Canada, the US and the UK in the late 1800s and early 1900s. She retired in 1909 to Vancouver and was welcomed as a celebrity. There she reconnected with Su-á-pu-luck/Capilano. She continued her writing by publishing local stories related to her by her friend in the *Daily Province*'s weekly Saturday magazine.[7]

Although the stories now circulate without political undertones, at the time of their publication, there was a definite agenda of resistance. Only a few years after the 1906 delegation, in a paper which often wrote about Su-á-pu-luck/Capilano as a troublemaker who incited unrest, Johnson used her celebrity status to distribute his stories that included Indigenous place names. For example, "The Two Sisters" tells the story of the north shore mountain peaks, which had been recently renamed "The Lions"; she also recounted the transformation of landmarks by χals, the transformer being, and she wrote other important stories that strategically grounded local Indigenous peoples in this physical and historical place that was rapidly also becoming Vancouver. She referred to Su-á-pu-luck/Capilano as her "tillicum" — a Chinook jargon word for friend, and his persona in the stories is one of a kind local guide. As Johnson was greatly admired by the settler population of Vancouver, it is likely that Adele Seymour and her husband read her columns, which aimed to centre Squamish ways of knowing.

Meanwhile, provincially the land title and reserve allocation problems continued. In 1907, the Nisga'a created Nisga'a Land Committee — the first effort by BC Indigenous people to create a politically recognizable organization to deal with government. In 1908, Premier Richard McBride suspended reserve surveys because of federal/provincial disagreements over land allocations (eventually resulting in the joint McKenna/ McBride Commission, which travelled throughout the province from 1911 to 1913). In 1909, the Cowichan people sent a delegation to the federal government and coastal groups created the Indian Rights Association. Interior southern Salish groups formed Interior Tribes of British Columbia. As this quick listing demonstrates, while levels of colonial government disagreed, Indigenous peoples across the province were organizing individually as well as collectively against the theft of their lands. The final years before Adele Seymour sold the land to the City of Vancouver were a time of intensifying struggle over the size of reserve lands and continuing Indigenous title, both locally and throughout the province.

And now we finally come to the moment when the land title changes from private ownership to park land. On February 13, 1909, Adele Seymour sold the lot of land that she had bought in 1892 for $3,300 to the City of Vancouver for $26,500 (about eight times what she had paid for it). Why that lot in particular was desirable is related to the original resident of the large mansion that still stands half a block away from the park. This was the geologist and professor Edward Odlum, who along with a few other neighbours created the Grandview Progress Association in 1907 (later known as the Grandview Ratepayers Association, GRA) shortly after the neighbourhood of Grandview was established. They met every second Tuesday at Odlum's house on Grant and Commercial and immediately began sending resolutions to City Council regarding the necessity of bridge building, street improvement and sewer extensions. In February 1908, the group began asking the city to retain grounds for a "Park and pleasure grounds."[8] There are no minutes recorded for 1909 — either they stopped meeting or they stopped recording their meetings. This may have been because they were busy supporting the city's purchase

Victoria Park, 1917, City of Vancouver Archives. Reference code: AM1535-: CVA 99-348, photographer Stuart Thomson

of the land. However, in the Parks Board minutes from 1908–1911, there are many details of letters sent by the GRA with regard to improvements to nearby Clark Park (April 20, 1908). After the acquisition of a few plots of land in 1909, the Parks Board had to figure out how to make the lands into parks and to decide on the purpose of these parks. A year after the city acquired the area that was then known as Grandview Park, the purpose of the park was still not settled, and the board directed the Grandview Ratepayers Association to "obtain the wishes of the residents" regarding whether the land would be athletic grounds or a pleasure park.[9] As the same people who had been advocating for a pleasure or garden park sat on the GRA, it is not surprising that just over a week later the board decided, on the basis of a report from the GRA and Odlum, to create a lawn and make use of it for pleasure only (Steele 1988: 215).[10] It was also around this time that the Parks Board renamed many of their holdings, and the name Grandview Park was changed to Victoria Park (Steele 1988: 215).

The work of constructing the park proceeded, but the Parks Board ran out of money for landscaping. In the summer of 1911, the GRA was still suggesting improvements to the park, in the form of creeping ivy to be planted over the rock formed entrances.[11] The next month the Parks Board decided to ask the neighbourhood associations in Grandview and Kitsilano to provide the plants for the recently opened parks. The board agreed that a fountain for the centre of Grandview Park would "add greatly to its ornament," but stated that they could not pay for it.[12] Within a month, the GRA notified the Parks Board that the fountain, shrubs and flowers would all be donated (Steele 1988: 216).[13] The controversy over the use of the park — either for athletics or "pleasure" — is one that is well-documented in the development of urban parks, and it's not surprising that there was also debate about who would have regular access to these twenty-two lots of land and for what purposes.

So, it was through Odlum's leadership that the land passed from private ownership by settlers to publicly held lands for pleasurable use by neighbourhood residents. Of all of the streets named after the prominent citizens, Odlum's is the least imposing — a short street running along the boundary of residential and light industry at the bottom of a steep hill down from Commercial Drive. This street is, however, the most connected to the person in terms of locality. Odlum did not live on that street, but he did live nearby, and he used his influence to create a neighbourhood with services that would help him enjoy his property — which was steps away from the land that became the park. I often think of him as I walk past his mansion, now turned into a housing co-op, and how his leadership with the Grandview Ratepayers Association continues to reverberate as people move into the neighbourhood and aim to "improve" it to their liking.

While these local concerns over the use of this small piece of land played out in the neighbourhood association and the municipal governance system, Indigenous peoples throughout the province continued their struggles to have their land title and resource rights respected. In 1910, Prime Minister Wilfrid Laurier stopped in Kamloops, BC, while on his re-election campaign, and he was met by Indigenous leaders who gave him a letter titled the "Laurier Memorial," which explained their discontent with the reserve system and the infringement on their rights. He was sympathetic to their cause, telling the Nisga'a that only the British Privy Council in London could settle the issue of title and apparently promised to get them a hearing, but his government was defeated in 1911 (Ray 2016: 323). Along with the Society of Friends of the Indians of British Columbia (formed in 1910 by Arthur O'Meara to provide financial and political support for Indigenous causes), Indigenous leaders prepared a petition to London, relying on the Royal Proclamation of 1763 to justify their case, which to reiterate, affirms Indigenous title and had been first the British and then Canadian guideline for treaty negotiations for over a hundred and forty-seven years. As urban development continued, pressure on Indigenous peoples within range of Victoria and Vancouver also increased. In 1911, the Lekwungen Nation (formerly known as the Songhees) were pressured into selling their reserve lands (Barman 2007: 6). Shortly after this, in 1912, a royal commission was organized to settle the differences between the federal and provincial governments regarding the size of reserve lands. Known as the McKenna-McBride Commission, it had five members, none of whom were Indigenous, and had no mandate to consider Indigenous title, self-governance or treaty negotiations. It could only increase or decrease the size of reserves.

The commission travelled the province from 1913 to 1916, and the Nisga'a and others initially boycotted the process because they were concerned it would interfere with their land claims (Ray 2016: 322). On June 24, 1913, the commissioners visited the Musqueam reserve at the mouth of the Fraser River. Susan Roy explains how the Musqueam adapted their traditions of visual displays of specific families' house posts and objects of power in the church building repurposed for the meeting in order to communicate with the commissioners the continuation of their history and their genealogical assertion of land titles and resource privileges. Charlie qiyəplenəxʷ spoke to them about the original reserve boundaries, which James Douglas had agreed to in the early 1860s and which had been reduced twice already without consultation. Johnny xʷəyxʷayələq also produced items representing the British Crown, understood by the Musqueam to be part of their diplomatic relations with the queen (Roy 2016: 72–9). While the commission was still under way, in 1913, the resident families of the Kitsilano Reserve, on the west side of Vancouver, were pressured into selling, the people removed by barge and the buildings burnt to the ground. This was all part of the "improvement" of the city that settlers such as Odlum and others involved in civic organizations energetically took up at the time.

In 1916, the Allied Tribes of British Columbia (ATBC) was formed in order to resist further losses of lands, and days later the McKenna-McBride Commission issued its report, which expanded some reserve lands in remote areas, but "cut off" lands in southern BC. The provincial government did nothing for two years, before finally asking the ATBC for their reaction. Despite their complete rejection of the recommendations, the provincial government passed them in 1920 (Ray 2016: 323–25). ATBC resistance and organizing continued on throughout the 1920s, until Duncan Campbell Scott, the deputy superintendent of Indian Affairs, drafted an amendment to the Indian Act — section 141 — which barred Indigenous peoples from soliciting funds to hire lawyers for land claims unless the government approved. This stayed in effect until 1951, when the act was amended again (326).

Despite my knowledge of the unfair practices of the Canadian government, this barring from legal land claims just as the Indigenous organizing was become more expansive and effective is jarring to read about. Along with the refusal to follow British practices regarding the acknowledgment of Indigenous land title for treaty negotiations that were part of the province's origin, the creation of a law that required Indigenous peoples to get government permission to file land claims against that same government positions the legal system as a kangaroo court.

The patch of land that became Victoria Park was developed throughout the rest of the twentieth century to include large trees offering shade and shelter on the perimeter, a pathway winding through the middle, nighttime lighting, public washroom facilities, bocce ball runs and playground equipment. After World War Two, with the influx of Italians fleeing the rise of fascism in Europe, the neighbourhood became known as Little Italy, and the park, despite the official signage, became much more well known as Bocce Ball Park. Parks Board records over these years document tensions around the use of the park for drinking, requests for the addition of night lighting, demands to close the nearby liquor store early and suggestions of posting of park rules in Italian. And throughout this time, Indigenous peoples continued to resist the taking of their lands and discriminatory policies. When it was no longer legal to file land claims, coastal groups united to protect fishing and hunting rights, the largest of these, the Native Brotherhood of British Columbia (NBBC), being formed in the north in 1931. When the federal government threatened to tax Indigenous commercial fishing operations, southern coastal groups also joined. After the war, the NBBC and other groups effectively organized to influence a 1951 revision of the Indian Act, most significantly lifting the ban on legal representation for land claims as well as public performances and ceremonies.

In the 1960s, 1970s and 1980s, as civil rights protests and cultural upheaval transformed power relations, the American Indian Movement as well as local and international Indigenous organizing brought about the inclusion of Aboriginal rights in section 35 of the Canadian Constitution and the creation of the United Nations Declaration on the Rights of Indigenous Peoples. This list of more recent actions, following the descriptions of Indigenous organizing throughout the late nineteenth and early twentieth centuries, should be enough to understand that the assertion of "unceded, traditional and ancestral territory" and the right to steward it in the present day cannot be de-historicized as a new movement.

Settler colonial ignorance and segregation from Indigenous peoples and ideas means that when a direct action gets media attention — such as the Kanehsatà:ke blockades of Oka development or the round dances that took place all over the country during Idle No More — it is often considered an isolated incident rather than part of a continuum of resistance that has been ongoing ever since colonial governments were able to legislate and apply policies of cultural genocide. As I have demonstrated by following the history of the land title changes to this small park, Indigenous resistance has been as continuous as it has been continuously, willfully ignored by settlers and newcomers who trade in property title and accrue profit from the extraction of value and resources from the land. This is an imaginary creation of both private property and the idea of a government administrated "commons" in a place that, if it has any legal basis for existence at all, must follow the established law of treaty negotiation for access to Indigenous lands. There has been a modern treaty process underway in BC since 1993; however, it is fraught with expectations over the extinguishing of Indigenous title in return for certain benefits.

But parks might be a place where we have room to think differently. In June 2014, following up on the declaration of the Year of Reconciliation in Vancouver, City Council unanimously voted to acknowledge that the city sits on unceded territory: "Underlying all other truths spoken during the Year of Reconciliation is the truth that the modern city of Vancouver was founded on the traditional territories of the Musqueam, Squamish and Tsleil-Waututh First Nations and that these territories were never ceded through treaty, war or surrender." On January 12, 2016, the Vancouver Parks Board approved eleven recommendations to move forward with the Truth and Reconciliation Commission's calls to action. These include the adoption of UNDRIP, the review of monuments and memorials to assure integration of Indigenous histories and a continuation of the "precedent setting intergovernmental approach to the future stewardship of Stanley Park and other relevant lands" (weaving 2016).

It is significant that the municipal governance of lands that are held (theoretically) in common for public use is one place that seems to be taking redress for cultural genocidal policies seriously. Now, in era of global warming, with continually strengthening Indigenous political, legal and ecological leadership, in a city that has acknowledged it is on unceded territory, non-Indigenous people who live on this land cannot pretend ignorance any longer. The task now is to collaborate with local Indigenous leaders to create responsible relations, which must include the actual decolonization of stolen lands. City parks in Vancouver, which are lands already held in common by an organization that has acknowledged the untenable nature of its land holdings, are the place to start this process. And perhaps a first step would be an effort to add meaning to the name Victoria Park, which includes the ten years of Indigenous gatherings in the late nineteenth century on the queen's birthday that were an effort hold settler colonial governments accountable. Making reparations for benefitting from land theft and cultural genocide will be a confusing and difficult process — one that we could call "un-settling" — but it is the necessary way to continue to respect the relationships we all have with the lands that we call home. Being comfortable with not knowing is something that newcomers and settlers on this land need to accept,

Victoria Park, day 138, May 18, 2015, Victoria Day. Photo by Daisy Couture

rather than relying on falsified documents of illegitimate title that give a mistaken understanding of property relations. The fear of losing the place one considers home may also be a way for settlers to develop empathy for Indigenous peoples, who have lived with this for generations now.

I want to emphasize why I've been discussing this "patch of grass" in the context of this long and circuitous history. In some ways it might seem a bit arbitrary — some of the dates of the land title exchanges line up neatly with Indigenous actions of refusal but not all of them. The stories behind the names of the land title holders do inform us of the landscape we live in and add meanings to the street names that may cause continuing reflection. The main reason, though, is because this is the place where we've lived for so long. It's a place that feels personal and connected — and if this work of settler self-decolonizing is going to happen, it has to be personalized in order for it to cause changes to ways of knowing and being. This is true for our small family and the friends and relations we have built up in our time living next to the park. After all of this, I still believe that our emotional attachment to our home and our memories of times spent in the park are valuable, and by living here even for this short time, we have added to the understanding of this land in some small way. And while honouring our connection to this land, we also need to take responsibility for how our inheritance of the pleasurable use that created this access is directly a result of ancestral actions of moving ever forward while discounting the visual, audible, embodied and documented presence of Indigenous peoples' relations to the land. If we are to stay here we have to understand who we are walking alongside and what other sort of future we might be able to create together.

FORWARD!

The first time I was compelled to think critically about the relationship between parks and colonial dispossession was back in the early 2000s. I was a recently minted graduate of the University of Alberta, having relocated from East Vancouver, where I had been living off and on for the previous five or so years. I had moved to Edmonton to distance myself from an unhealthy cycle of shit wage-work rendered slightly more tolerable by an enthusiastic commitment to booze and drug use. I thought that giving a crack at school might help facilitate my escape. Why I would think such a thing, I have no idea. I demonstrated no skill for academics in high school — my racist classmates and teachers drilled that out of me at an early age — and I failed out of an equally hostile and mediocre community college immediately after that. My Alberta move was thus a bit of a gamble. The university at the time had a bridging program for adult Native students, which enabled me to circumvent the lofty admission requirements that the civilian settler population had to meet. The rub was, anyone accessing the program was put on "probation," which meant that we could only take a maximum of three courses in which we had to meet a certain grade-point average. I can't recall what that average was, although I do remember my feeling of dread because there was no way in hell I thought I could ever meet it. If you managed to meet the average, you were in.

Because I applied the workplace skill I developed in the art of tardiness to my university admissions application, class selection was severely limited: some bullshit course on dinosaurs where we spent much of our time close-watching *Jurassic Park*; a philosophy course on brains-as-computers where sectarian old white men yelled at each other through the books they wrote; and a first-year Native studies course were what I got stuck with. What seemed to be a lacklustre start to my university experience ended up serving me well in the end. I digested a useless yet significant amount of information about dinosaurs, I got a taste for philosophy and theory in the brain course, and I began to slowly develop a militancy in relation to Indigenous peoples and struggles in Native studies — again, a politics that was violently shamed out of me at a very early age. It was this newly minted politicized version of myself that returned to Vancouver and started to help organize with folks against then premier Gordon Campbell's Liberal Party–led racist tirade against Aboriginal rights in the province.

As those living in BC then will remember, Premier Campbell's most belligerent assault on Indigenous rights came in the form of a public "referendum" on the nature and scope of land claim negotiations between BC First Nations and the Crown, otherwise known as the "modern treaty" process. Unlike many other regions in Canada, there were very few historical treaties signed between Indigenous peoples and the state in BC (save the Douglas Treaties on Vancouver Island and Treaty 8 in the northeastern corner of the province). From the perspective of the Crown, the purpose of signing treaties with Indigenous peoples was to secure state sovereignty over what were previously the self-governed territories of Indigenous nations through a process called "extinguishment." Extinguishment was thought to be the most expedient way to expropriate Indigenous land title for the twin purposes of colonial settlement and capitalist development on Indigenous peoples' lands. In BC and many places across the north, these mechanisms of legalized land theft were never implemented, thus leaving legal and economic uncertainty over the unceded territories in question. Who owns the land in such circumstances? What are the rules that guide settlement and development in these places? Rich white guys tend to like answers to these questions before they invest too heavily in development projects, especially in liberal states like Canada, so that angry Indians don't legally have a leg to stand on when they disrupt profit margins by blocking roads and flows of resource capital hemorrhaging from their traditional territories. Thus, the so-called "modern treaty" process in BC was established in 1991 to finish the job that historical treaties were implemented to do in other jurisdictions.

Even though the process was put in place to once and for all divest

Indigenous peoples of their legal interests in land, this wasn't enough for Gordon Campbell and his governing Liberal Party. Campbell was always quite bad at maintaining the delicate balance between his social conservative contempt for First Nations and his neoconservative love of the market. Indeed, it was his racist disdain for First Nations and their rights that led him to call a referendum on what was otherwise a perfectly neoliberal approach to colonial land dispossession in the province.

By now you should be wondering what the hell this story has to do with the collective political meditation offered by Matt, Selena, Sadie and Daisy in *On This Patch of Grass: City Parks on Occupied Land*. One of the most important challenges grappled with in the book deals with the largely unproblematized juxtaposition between the unqualified "good" of lands deemed public or common, and the "bad" of those legislated as private. In popular discourse, parks, the authors suggest, are often represented as the former — as sites of uncontested natural beauty, diversity, conservation, and inclusion. Yet in the settler-colonial context of historically layered land theft, the normative juxtaposition that structures the public-private binary loses much of its critical force, and this is what I find so important about the book, on the one hand, and what I found so productively illuminating/frustrating about the racist treaty referendum, on the other. The referendum was publicly distributed in 2002 and consisted of eight vague, emotionally manipulative statements that the citizenry was called on to answer with a simple "yes" or "no." The statements ranged from the legally particular — asking Joe Citizen to weigh in on what *he* thinks ought to be scope of jurisdiction for self-governing *First Nations* — to the purposely ambiguous and misleading — essentially asking an ignorant non-Native public whether First Nations ought to pay taxes (assuming erroneously that we don't already). The most affectively sinister statements, however — and the ones which I remember garnering so much news time and public debate — tapped into the emotional juggernaut of private property and public lands, and to the relationship of both to the sacrosanct rights of colonial citizenship. "Private property should not be expropriated for treaty settlements" and "Parks and protected areas should be maintained for the use and benefit of all British Columbians" — yes or no? Said differently, if BC and Canada don't limit the "special" rights of First Nations in the treaty process, Indians are going to take *your* property and deny you access to *our* land. And the debate raged on in ignorance.

Not much prior to 2002 I saw parks as places to read books and drink beers. Indeed, more likely than not, I was probably one of the diverse characters that turn up in the pages of *On This Patch of Grass*. After 2002, however, parks took on a political significance to me. I began to see them as spaces of political affect and contestation that could be manipulated quite easily toward neo-colonial ends, in much the same way that property rights to one's house or cottage or ranch have historically done in a more open and straightforward manner. In the settler-colonial context of historically layered land dispossession, the private-public binary represents two sides of the same coin, and for this reason we owe a debt of gratitude to Matt, Selena, Sadie, and Daisy for raising these critically important issues and staging such an important, nuanced conversation on the politics of the commons in the wake of colonial occupation.

Mahsi cho.

> — *Glen Sean Coulthard, teacher of political theory and*
> *Indigenous politics at the University of British Columbia.*
> *He is Yellowknives Dene.*

NOTES

1: CITY PARKS ON OCCUPIED LAND

1. Also known in the Canadian media as the "Oka Crisis." It's worth taking a minute to contextualize our present moment: the events of the summer of 1990 were built on the increasing militancy throughout the 1980s, such as the Constitution Express, the Innu Occupation of military sites in Goose Bay (Labrador), the Lubicon Lake Cree boycott of the 1988 Calgary Olympics, Temagami Nation's blockades against development, and Indigenous resistance to the Meech Lake Accord in 1990, and all together these events triggered the Royal Commission on Aboriginal peoples (RCAP), 1991–96 (Coulthard 2012). Following the RCAP's recommendations 1.10.1 to 1.10.3 and as a direct result a court-ordered Indian Residential School Agreement class action settlement in 2006, the Truth and Reconciliation Commission of Canada (TRC) on Indian Residential Schools was established. The TRC commissioners issued ninety-four calls to action in June 2015 that demand redress and actions to support reconciliation at all levels of government; in the education, legal and health care systems; and in how the history of Canada is commemorated. As we write this in the summer of 2018, ten calls are complete, fifteen are underway, twenty-five have had projects proposed and forty-four have not yet started (CBC Interactives 2018).

2. You will note our use of the words "settler" and "visitor." They are loaded terms that have come under rightful scrutiny. The term "settler" refers to non-Indigenous residents on Indigenous territory who are afforded their legitimacy by the settler colonial state; "visitor" is more ambiguous but, without a clear ongoing invitation to be here by a host, this term also blurs into occupation. They are accurate in some ways, but they also obscure critical differentiations among non-Indigenous inhabitants and the routes by which they came to be here and tend to reduce the entire population to a simple Indigenous/settler binary. The landscape is far more complicated and nuanced than that, with vast differences in access to resources and privileges. To call refugees, for example, who have escaped horrendous circumstances "settlers" or "visitors" ignores the violence of their displacements and expulsions. Similarly, naming Black people in North America as "settlers" papers over a history of slavery and violent relocations. We acknowledge the complexities of the terms and note the instabilities of both words. Right now, settler and visitor are the best descriptions of our family. It is also worth highlighting that we are a white family, a

reality that intersects and inflects our settler status but is not synonymous with it. It is important here to note that there are many colonialisms. Here in North America the mode is best described as "settler colonialism," where colonial settlers come to stay and do not leave, but this is just one mode of colonial rationalities.

2: A BETTER LANDSCAPE

1. From 1910 through 1961, for example, the Vancouver Gun Club conducted an every-Saturday-morning Stanley Park crow-hunt, trying (futilely) to exterminate the "winged vermin" who were transgressing in the Park (Kheraj 2013: 131).
2. Ivvavik National Park in the Yukon, Torngat Mountains National Park in Labrador, Thaydene Nene National Park in the Northwest Territories are all well-known examples, but there are many other versions in most other provinces. There are a few other affiliated terms: cooperative management, collaborative management, community management, joint management — but they all mean basically the same thing, or are in the same constellation of reforms.

4: THE PARK GOERS

1. While Greg Younging's *Elements of Indigenous Style* advises italicizing Indigenous words in English language publications as a way to interrupt the practice of Indigenous languages being swallowed up by English (e.g., canoe), we have taken a different approach in this text. We follow the method used by Noenoe K. Silva in her book *Aloha Betrayed,* in which she does not italicize Hawaiian words because they are from the language Indigenous to the land under discussion. She and other scholars deploy this method as a resistance to making Indigenous languages appear foreign (2004: 13). While this can be disorienting, it also demands that the reader make an effort to learn Indigenous words and meanings.

5: TITLING VICTORIA PARK

1. All information on land title transfers comes from West Coast Title search documents on "Lot E (Explanatory Plan 15137) Block B of Block 137 District Lot 264A Plans 305 and 1771" conducted by Marie Resurreccion.
2. For a contemporary engagement with the significance of the proclamation see the short film "250 Years: Honor Your Words," produced by Sámi /Kainai filmmaker Elle-Máijá Tailfeathers in 2013, shortly after the Idle No More insurgence began. <https://vimeo.com/76246943>.
3. The top five landowners, in descending order, with the estimated worth of their holdings in 1887: CPR $1,000,000; Hastings Saw Mill $250,000; Oppenheimer Bros. Real Estate $125,000; Brighouse & Hailstone $100,000; Dr. I.W. Powell $75,000 (MacDonald 1977: 18).
4. This is the only land title purchaser of whom I can find no trace. He may have been

a local citizen as there are records of John Philip Matheson and his son Robert who were prominent architects who designed many English Tudor style buildings locally. Robert Matheson's company, Matheson and Townley was a major architecture firm which built many houses in Shaughnessy as well as City Hall in 1935, but there is no mention of Malcolm in the city archives, or other local history texts.

5. The pamphlet on Seymour is the source of all his biographical info, City of Vancouver Archives (hereafter CoV Archives) AM1519-: PAM 1967-224 <http://searcharchives. vancouver.ca/joseph-richard-seymour-founder-of-scottish-rite-masonry-and-royal-order-of-scotland-in-british-columbia>.\; J.R. Seymour Druggist CoV archives file AM54-S23-2 <http://searcharchives.vancouver.ca/seymour-j-r-druggist>. There is not enough space in this short place-focused essay to fully examine the linkages between the city's land-title-owning business class and the fraternal order of the Masons, in particular the Scottish Rite Masonry (which had a particular emphasis on performance and role playing as part of their self-improvement program). It is worth mentioning that Israel Powell, also one of the land's previous owners, was also a well-known leader involved with establishing the Masons in BC.

6. A trade language spoken by multiple Indigenous groups throughout the Pacific northwest.

7. These columns were eventually collected by her supporters and published as *Legends of Vancouver* in 1911, as a way to generate an income for her when she was ill with breast cancer.

8. "Minute Book of the Grandview Progress Association, 1907-1910." Edward Odlum Fonds. CoV Archives. A.M. 190, file 2, 513-0-10. <http://searcharchives.vancouver. ca/edward-odlum-fonds Grandview Progress Association 1907-1910>.

9. "Parks Board — Board Meeting Minutes" 1888-1997. CoV archives. Series S76. 1 April 1910. <http://searcharchives.vancouver.ca/park-board-board-meeting-minutes>.

10. "Parks Board — Board Meeting Minutes" 1888-1997. CoV archives. Series S76. 12 April 1910. <http://searcharchives.vancouver.ca/park-board-board-meeting-minutes>.

11. "Parks Board — Board Meeting Minutes" 1888-1997. CoV archives. Series S76. 23 August 1911. <http://searcharchives.vancouver.ca/park-board-board-meeting-minutes>.

12. "Parks Board — Board Meeting Minutes" 1888-1997. CoV archives. Series S76. 27 September 1911. <http://searcharchives.vancouver.ca/park-board-board-meeting-minutes>.

13. "Parks Board — Board Meeting Minutes" 1888-1997. CoV archives. Series S76. 25 October 1911. <http://searcharchives.vancouver.ca/park-board-board-meeting-minutes>.

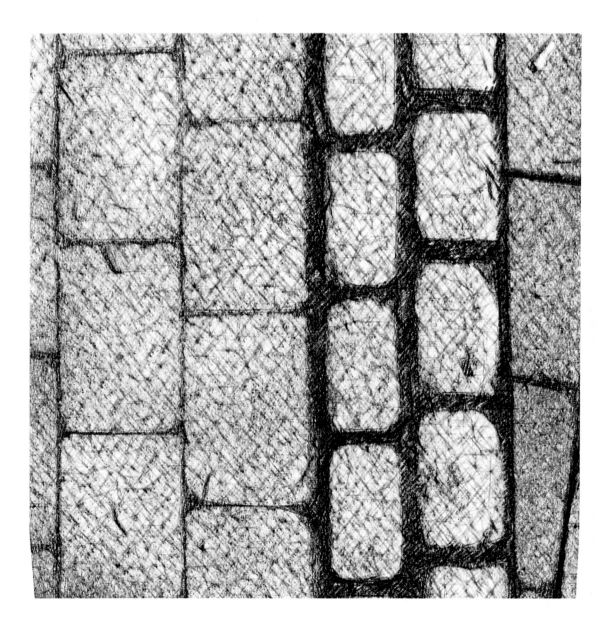

REFERENCES

Arola, Adam. 2011. "Responses to *This Is Not A Peace Pipe: Towards a Critical Indigenous Philosophy* by Dale Turner: Dialogue and Identity, Worries about Word Warriors?" *APA Newsletters, Newsletter on Indigenous Philosophy*, 10, 2 (Spring).

Barman, Jean. 2007. "Erasing Indigenous Indigeneity in Vancouver." *BC Studies*, 155.

Beveridge, Charles E. 2000 "Olmsted: His Essential Theory." National Association for Olmstead Parks. <www.olmsted.org/the-olmsted-legacy/olmsted-theory-and-design-principles/olmsted-his-essential-theory>.

Brecht, Bertolt. 1995 [1936]. "From Alienation Effects in Chinese Acting: The A-Effect." In Richard Drain (ed.), *Twentieth Century Theatre: A Sourcebook*,. NY and London: Routledge.

Carter, Jill. 2015. "Discarding Sympathy, Disrupting Catharsis: The Mortification of Indigenous Flesh as Survivance-Intervention." *Theatre Journal*, 67.3.

CBC Interactives. 2018. "Beyond 94." <https://newsinteractives.cbc.ca/longform-single/beyond-94?&cta=1>.

City of Vancouver. 2010. Park Bylaws. <http://vancouver.ca/files/cov/parks-control-bylaw-July06-2010.pdf>.

City of Vancouver Parks and Recreation. 2018. "Wildlife." <http://vancouver.ca/parks-recreation-culture/wildlife.aspx>.

"City of Vancouver Population." 2007. VPL Social Sciences Division, 20 March. <https://web.archive.org/web/20070614201558/http://www.vpl.ca/branches/LibrarySquare/soc/pdfs/QF_Population_BC_Vancouver.pdf>.

Coulthard, Glen. 2012. "#Idlenomore in Historical Context." Decolonization: Indigeneity, Education & Society blog. December 24. <https://decolonization.wordpress.com/2012/12/24/idlenomore-in-historical-context/>.

Dangeli, Mique'l. 2015. "Dancing Sovereignty: Protocol and Politics in Northwest Coast First Nations Dance." Unpublished doctoral dissertation, University of British Columbia.

Du Bois, W.E.B. 1920. "The Souls of White Folk." *Darkwater*. <http://www.gutenberg.org/files/15210/15210-h/15210-h.htm>.

Falcon, Paulette. 1991. "'if the evil ever occurs': The 1873 Married Women's Property Act: Law, Property and Gender Relations in 19th Century British Columbia." MA thesis, University of British Columbia.

Fenge, Terry, and Jim Aldridge (eds.). 2015. *Keeping Promises: The Royal Proclamation of 1763, Aboriginal Rights and Treaties in Canada*. Montreal & Kingston: McGill-Queen's University Press.

Greer, Evans F. 1967 "Joseph Richard Seymour: Founder of Scottish Rite Masonry and Royal Order of Scotland in British Columbia." Canadian Masonic Research Association.

Harris, Cole. 2002. *Making Native Space: Colonialism, Resistance and Reserves in British Columbia.* Vancouver: UBC Press.

Heller, Chaia. 1999. *Ecology of Everyday Life: Rethinking the Desire for Nature.* Montreal: Black Rose Books.

Indigenous Climate Action. 2016. "Standing with Standing Rock Edmonton." <https://www.facebook.com/indigenousclimateaction/videos/1783260565258591/?autoplay_reason=all_page_organic_allowed&video_container_type=4&video_creator_product_type=0&app_id=6628568379&live_video_guests=0>.

Jacobs, Jane. 1961. *The Death and Life of Great American Cities.* New York: Vintage.

Johnson, Pauline. 1911. *Legends of Vancouver.* Vancouver & Victoria, BC: David Spencer Limited.

Justice, Daniel Heath. 2018. "Creative Overview." <http://danielheathjustice.com/creative/>.

Kheraj, Sean. *Inventing Stanley Park: An Environmental History.* Vancouver: UBC Press, 2013.

MacDonald, Norbert. 1977. "The Canadian Pacific Railway and Vancouver's Development to 1900." *BC Studies,* 35.

McKay, Fergus, and Emily Caruso. 2004. "Indigenous Lands or National Parks." *Cultural Survival Quarterly Magazine,* 28.1. <www.culturalsurvival.org/publications/cultural-survival-quarterly/indigenous-lands-or-national-parks>.

Moreton-Robinson, Aileen. 2015. *The White Possessive.* Minneapolis: University of Minnesota Press.

Ray, Arthur. 2016. *An Illustrated History of Canada's Native Peoples.* Montreal & Kingston: McGill-Queen's University Press.

___. 1999. "Treaty 8: A British Columbia Anomaly." *BC Studies,* 123.

Roy, Susan. 2016. *These Mysterious People: Shaping History and Archaeology in a Northwest Coast Community.* Montreal & Kingston: McGill-Queen's University Press.

Royal Commission on Aboriginal Peoples. 1996. Library and Archives Canada. <https://www.bac-lac.gc.ca/eng/discover/aboriginal-heritage/royal-commission-aboriginal-peoples/Pages/introduction.aspx>.

Silva, Noenoe K. 2004. *Alohoa Betrayed: Native Hawaiian Resistance to American Colonialism.* Duke University Press.

Simpson, Leanne Betasamosake. 2013. "Restoring Nationhood: Addressing Land Dispossession in the Canadian Reconciliation Discourse." Lecture, SFU Woodward's, November 13 <https://www.youtube.com/watch?v=SGUcWih74Ic>.

Snyders, Tom, and Jennifer O'Rourke. 2000. *Namely Vancouver.* Vancouver: Gibson Library Connection.

Steele, R. Mike. 1988. *The Vancouver Board of Parks and Recreation: The First 100 Years: An Illustrated Celebration.* Vancouver: Vancouver Board of Parks and Recreation.

Stevenson, Marc. 2004. "Decolonizing Co-Management in Northern Canada." *Cultural Survival Quarterly Magazine,* 28-1. <www.culturalsurvival.org/publications/cultural-survival-quarterly/decolonizing-co-management-northern-canada>.

Tailfeathers, Elle-Máijá. 2013. "250 Years: Honour Your Words." *Vimeo*. <https://vimeo.com/76246943 >.

Tennant, Paul. 1990. *Aboriginal People and Politics: The Indian Land Question in British Columbia, 1849–1989*. Vancouver: UBC Press.

"The province of British Columbia, Canada, its resources, commercial position and climate, and description of the new field opened up by the Canadian Pacific Railway." 1886. CoV archives PAM 1886-4 <http://searcharchives.vancouver.ca/province-of-british-columbia-canada-its-resources-commercial-position-and-climate-and-description-of-new-field-opened-up-by-canadian-pacific-railway-with-information-for-intending-settlers-based-on-personal-investigations-of-writer-and>.

Thor Carlson, Keith. 2010. *The Power of Place; the Problem of Time: Aboriginal Identity and Historical Consciousness in the Cauldron of Colonialism*. Toronto: University of Toronto Press.

___. 2005. "Rethinking Dialogue and History: The King's Promise and the 1906 Aboriginal Delegation to London." *Native Studies Review*, 16, 2.

Tuck, Eve, and K. Wayne Yang. 2012. "Decolonization Is Not a Metaphor." *Decolonization: Indigeneity, Education & Society*, 1,1.

Twombley, Robert (ed.). 2010. *Frederick Law Olmsted: Essential Texts*. New York: WW Norton.

Underwood, Jaqui. 2010. "When the World Was Young." In Donald E. Waite (ed.), *Vancouver Exposed: A History in Photographs*. Maple Ridge, BC: Waite Publishing.

weaving, jil. 2016. "Truth and Reconciliation Commission Calls to Action: Recommendation." *Vancouver Board of Parks and Recreation*. January 6. <http://parkboardmeetings.vancouver.ca/2016/20160111/REPORT-TRCCallsToAction-20160111.pdf>.

Vancouver Daily World. 1902. "Sale of Land for Taxes." 11 June. Vancouver, BC.

Younging, Greg. 2018. *Elements of Indigenous Style*. Brush Education Inc.

INDEX